Child Custody
A Mother's Issue

One Woman's Personal Story and
Guide of the Legal System and
Other Options

M.J KAIN

MJK Productions
Marysville Washington

MJK Productions
1242 State St. Suite I-139
Marysville WA 98270

All rights reserved.
Copyright © 1997 by M.J. Kain
All rights reserved
Library of Congress Catalog Card Number: 97-92938
ISBN: 0-9655846-1-5
No part of this book may be reproduced or transmitted in any form or by any means, electronic, mechanical photocopying, recording, or otherwise. It may not be stored in or introduced into a retrieval system, without permission in writing from the publisher.

Printed in U.S.A

Acknowledgments

    I would like to thank my family and friends for their support and encouragement.. Paula, my neighbor, who took time to read my rough draft and gave me her honest opinion.
    To the ladies who gave me their time to explain how each of their facilitators offices work; Kathy Wheeler Clark County, and Linda Hutcheson Whatcom County.

    To Dispute Resolution Center for providing me with information on mediatation programs around the country.
    To Margaret D. Smith, editor, for her input, encouragment, and positive remarks.
    Thank you to the people who did last minute proof reading, Kevin and Laura, Jennifer, Tina, Heidi and Oleta.

Contents

Part 1: The Story
My personal account of my situation 1

Part 2: Reference
Attorneys 69
Disputing Custody 71
Mediation 79
Representing Yourself 82
Mediation Programs 92

Dear Reader:

This book shares my experience and opinions of options that may lead you to keeping personal issues; such as child custody, out of court. When you find a system that works, you must explore it thoroughly. Laws and the system can change on any day. Some of the things I talk about in this book may differ in your state. This book is sold with the understanding that the author is not engaged in rendering specific legal advice to any person.

Part One
The Story

Introduction
Why I Wrote

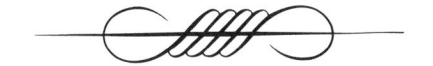

———⚜———

I began this book in my mind; retracing the steps of my life, experiences that led me to the custody dispute over my son. He was four years old at the time. A judge had awarded primary custodial care to my ex-boyfriend.

I was devastated. I was sure I was alone. How many mother's lose primary care of their child or children? Don't you have to have something wrong with you? Such as drug abuse or neglect?

In our society today, more and more women are becoming every other weekend mothers.

I wanted to take the story from my head, and put it down on paper. Talking with mothers going or who would be going, into custody disputes, persuaded me that I was right. I learned a lot from my judicial experience. I wish I knew then what I know now. Isn't that how it always is?

I wrote much of my private life, so you can see I'm an average woman, that has had some up and down times. I try to find the lesson in each happy or sad time that has happened in my life.

So, along with my personal story, I have touched on different ways the reader can help yourself; hopefully saving you money, time and bitter feelings that usually accompany a 'custody battle.'

I wonder if I lost full custody of my son, maybe, for the reason of being able to tell a story. Saying to you, "Hey, it's not all what it seems, be careful." I trusted others when I should have trusted myself the most.

The reference part of this book comes from my own experiences. They are my opinions. They won't work for everyone I suppose, but there are different ways to solve your situation, and you should know that.

I have changed everyone's name that was involved in this story. It is to protect my children, it is to protect my custody case. If you can relate to this story, I hope that you find it helpful, and learn some things.

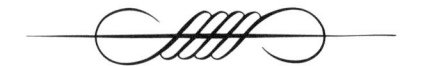

I became a statistic early in my life. I was a mother at age eighteen. In my life plan, that was not supposed to happen. I was going to graduate from highschool but had no desire for college.

In my senior year, I was working at a big-name department store at one of the malls. It was perfect. I was making quite a bit more than the minimum wage and had good benefits. That was going to be my start; get a good job, save some money, marry my boyfriend I had known through highschool, and buy a home.

We planned to travel, maybe buy a boat, and put children on hold until we had made a home and saved some money.

However life usually doesn't deliver what you expect. And if your plans do work as you wish, somewhere down the line, something happens to totally throw you in the other direction.

When I was two months into my unknown pregnancy, my boyfriend, William, was killed in an automobile accident. We had suspected I was pregnant, and he had suggested we go to the hospital and get the test done there. But I was almost finished with school and I was too afraid to know. We didn't have the chance to go together for the news. I took a home test a month after he was killed.

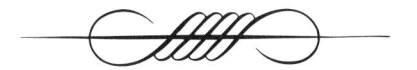

It was a rough pregnancy. I was huge and always uncomfortable. I dealt with William's death as if it hadn't happened. It was the defense part of my emotions, I think, to help me get through the months of pregnancy.

Early one morning in my ninth month, my water broke. A friend of mine drove me to the hospital, but after I was situated in my room, I asked her to leave. I didn't want anyone around, only the nurses.

My mother was called, and they told her my wishes. Labor wasn't starting, and contractions did not come, not even a minor one.

The nurses tried to help it along with petosin. They hooked me up to an IV, and soon the chemical began to take effect. After about thirty minutes, it was clear I was in trouble.

A contraction began but did not end. My stomach was pushing out and getting tighter by the second. A nurse got me off the petosin and replaced it with morphine, to bring me out of the contraction and rest my body for labor.

They hoped the contractions would start on their own from this effect. I was in and out of consciousness all night with strange dreams. A rainbow of color swirled in my head. I didn't remember where I was, but I felt safe.

The next afternoon, they started with the petosin again. This time it brought on regular contractions. After some time, I was sent to the labor room.

The delivery was a horrible experience. I was given an epidural to numb me waist down, but I still had the morphine trip in my head, not a good combination.

I wasn't very helpful in my pushing efforts. All I could see was this child coming out with a face looking just like William. It was frightening.

How could I have a baby without the father? It was hitting me now what was going on. My boyfriend was gone, and I was having a baby. Throughout the delivery, I became more confused. I thought I would pass out.

The baby was born, a girl, but no tears came from her. Several nurses rushed her away. I looked up from where I lay. A bed-size mirror had been lowered from the ceiling, for those who want to watch themselves give birth. I had asked that it be put up, but there it was still, and all I could see was blood everywhere.

In my daze I wondered if it was from the baby; maybe that was why she didn't cry. The doctor was stitching me, and all I could hear was mumbling. I strained to understand the voices but couldn't.

Then two nurses came in and spoke with the doctor. They all wore concerned looks on their faces. But then, their expressions changed as they wheeled me into a recovery room. They looked angry, then sad, and then a smile would appear. Was I hallucinating?

While in the hall, another nurse ran up to my side. "You had a girl; what's her name? What's her name?"

I couldn't feel my body. She wanted to know what? Louder, she said "What's the baby's name?"

I couldn't remember. I had one picked out, but I didn't know it at that point. I replied "Ruth. It's from the Bible."

I began to drift off. I was remembering the last stories I had been reading in the Bible. The name Ruth showed up many times. That was her name, although I hadn't considered it before. I was in a recovery bed now and was given more medication. I went into a deep, peaceful sleep.

A nurse woke me up. It had been a couple hours since the birth. I was a wreck. Now I was achy, and she needed to insert a catheter in me. My body seemed all misshapen, like a clump of molded clay.

My mother had visited and left me some flowers. I asked how the baby was, remembering how the nurses had taken her out of the room so quickly.

The nurse didn't look at me with her answer, "She's really sick. The staff is doing everything for her, though."

"You mean she could die? I asked anxiously, "You can tell me the truth." She pulled a wheelchair close to my bed.

She smiled at me,"A doctor will come in to talk to you about everything, I just need to get you to your room. Recovery is getting crowded, so we need your bed." I wondered why, because I sure didn't feel like moving, let alone being all recovered from delivery. When she got me to my room, I couldn't believe it. It was a private room with a view. How did I get that? I didn't ask but I appreciated it.

I got comfortable in my bed, and was trying to sort things out. I was still having a hard time keeping my thoughts straight.

A soft knock came from at door. A man in a long white coat appeared, "Hi, my name is Doctor Wilson. I know you must still be exhausted from everything, but we need to talk about some things."

I just stared at him as he continued. "Your baby is very sick. In basic terms, she's hemorrhaging in the stomach and her body is, for some reason, unable to form clots. She was also more discolored then normal, leading us to believe she had been without oxygen for some time. We've got an oxygen bubble surrounding her head, and a tube in her belly and one down her throat. Those are working on moving out the blood accumulation, keeping her clear."

I was stunned. I had no words. Death had come knocking again. Uh, excuse me, Lord, I thought, are you trying to make me lose my mind? I'm not sure I can handle all this.

Doctor Wilson gave a weak smile. "Another problem also appeared. With the stress of the hemorrhaging, there's also been kidney failure. And that's why I'm here. Among all the other stuff, I specialize in the kidneys. I didn't want to be the bearer of all this news. I'm sure it's quite a shock to you. How about if we talk later? I'll have more information. You get some rest, and I'll come back."

I started to think I should plan for the worst, that she wouldn't make it. I wanted her buried as close to her dad as possible, and I should make some plans for her to be blessed. Did I have to do this? No, instead I said a prayer. I wouldn't plan a funeral until that time actually came. I prayed, and asked God, "Do whatever you want, but guide me in the right direction." Then I slept. No dreaming, just deep sleep.

The next morning Doctor Wilson visited: "How are you feeling?"

I felt gross, all bloated and hadn't showered in a couple of days. "Oh, all right I guess. I'm still pretty weak though."

"Yes, I bet you are. I understand you had a lot of blood loss at delivery. Well, Ruth made it through the night with remarkable results."

"The internal bleeding has stopped, he continued, "It's really amazing. I have to admit to you that I've only seen three other cases like hers. Two died and the other has severe cerebral palsy. Ruth's not out of the woods yet, though. She's got a good heart, and she was full term, so those factors will work in her favor. She seems awfully strong, and she'll need to be."

So she's a fighter, I thought; I knew she'd make it. "Doctor Wilson, what are the chances of her recovery?"

"That's hard to say. Like I said before, there's only a few cases such as hers, and there are no records or studies for outcome. The lab is doing some blood work, also, just to make sure her levels are okay. We don't want her suffering some deficiency in that area."

The doctor left, and I thought how nice he was to keep me informed. It occurred to me that I hadn't seen or talked with my regular physician since the birth. I felt it was because of everything that had happened. Maybe she was in hiding, or maybe she was the one who pulled some strings and got me the nice room.

The third evening of my stay, I was feeling better. I had gotten to know my nurses. They were the same three, morning, afternoon and night. They were very friendly and helpful.

That night I was feeling more alert than usual. Maybe all the drugs were finally working their way out of my system. The nurse came in to check on me, and she must have noticed I was sitting upright in bed, rather than the usual curled-up position. "Would you like me to take you to the nursery to see your baby?" she asked.

My stomach did a flip with that question. "Yes, I would. I have to tell you I'm nervous though. Is that bad of me to feel that way?"

She smiled, "No, I don't think so. There's been a lot going on from what I understand, and I don't blame you. I'll go get you a wheelchair."

"No, I don't want one, I want to try to walk." So with her help, we went to visit the special care nursery. We walked in, and there were four babies. I searched for Ruth. The babies were obviously all premature. They were so small, almost not human-looking. One had its eyes taped closed and lay under a yellow light. The others were being attended to by nurses.

Another nurse came out from the back of the room. She touched me on my shoulder."Hi, you're here to see your baby, Ruth, right? She's right over here." We followed her. My nurse whispered, "I had to call to make sure it was okay we came over, so they are prepared for you."

There she was. She was huge, compared to the other babies in the room. I stood there in amazement. I had that baby? Whoa, no wonder I was in pain. Ruth was sleeping, there was no tube in her belly or mouth, just an IV hooked into her right arm.

I asked "How is she doing? I mean really, tell me how it's going for her."

Ruth's nurse smiled. "I was here when they brought her in. She's a total miracle. I just love her. We still have to watch her for recurring problems, but there haven't been any yet. It's still kind of early to tell, but she's doing well. When I left my shift that day, I wondered if she'd still be here when I was working again. I was so happy for her when I saw she was."

The nurse really had compassion for Ruth. I could see she was sincere. I touched Ruth's hand and she flinched. She looked really tired, just worn out. The nurse spoke again, "We hope that she'll start taking a bottle. That would be a great sign. I've tried a little this evening, but she wasn't interested."

I was happy to see Ruth was in good hands. I had become very tired just from this little venture. Thanking the nursery nurse for all her help, I went back to my room. I cried myself to sleep, so unsure of my future.

The morning nurse came in with my medication and vitamins for my anemia that had resulted from my delivery.

"You know you get to go home tomorrow morning; isn't that great?"

It wasn't. I didn't want to leave the hospital, my bed, the nurses. I had grown attached to them all.

"How come my regular doctor has never come to visit?" The nurse placed breakfast before me, "You mean the one who delivered? I don't know. Do you want me to call for her?"

"No thank you, I guess I don't need or really want to see her."

Doctor Wilson popped in again, "Hey, how are you doing? I hear you're going home tomorrow."

I nodded. "Okay, well I need to let you know Ruth has had a setback. The hemorrhaging hasn't come back, but the lab results show spinal meningitis. They did a spinal tap on her along with the blood and found a bacteria in the work."

"How deadly could that be, I asked.

"Well", said Dr. Wilson, "deadly. "We're going to continue antibiotics and see how it goes. Honestly, it's not something we want her to be dealing with. We'll have to wait it out."

I asked, "How do you get a bacteria like that?"

"Well, there are several that can cause the meningitis. It may be as simple as something you ate, then passed on through the placenta. There's been talk of deadly bacterias showing up in unpasteurized milks and cheeses. It may have well come from that, but it's something we can't be sure of."

Well, I knew Ruth would get through it, but with healthy results? I wasn't so sure. Either way, I knew I was the one that was responsible for her. I just had to get my mind straight and back to reality. I needed another nap and said a prayer before I slept.

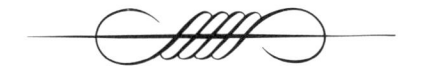

My mother was at my room to pick me up bright and early. I had dressed in a sweatshirt and sweats and I felt like I was going to cry. I really wanted to be back in my hospital gown and crawl back into my bed. The morning nurse came in to check on me. It wasn't the regular one, and I asked where she was.

"Well, she has to have a day off, she replied, I guess this is one of them." Well, maybe I was ready to leave, I thought. I don't want a whole day of new nurses, so it was an incentive to go.

I checked on Ruth. She was in a different nursery, under special care nonetheless. It was bigger. Babies had been there quite a few months recovering from their premature births. Ruth was the only baby there because of an illness.

I introduced myself to the nurse who would be caring for Ruth for that shift. I told her I would call later. Ruth was sleeping. I was told she would be doing a lot of that, because her body needed it.

I was sad to leave and didn't speak to my mother all the way home. I knew by leaving the hospital, I was entering a new phase of my life, something so unexpected, something so unplanned.

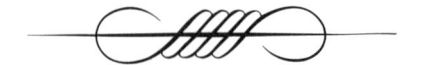

Meanwhile, still in the hospital, Ruth struggled for days, fighting off the bacteria. I visited every day, missing maybe two altogether because I was unable to get a ride to the hospital. Those two days, though, were filled with deep thinking, crying, and confusion. After that, the hospital was almost another home. I didn't long to be there as I did before. I didn't even go to my old room or speak to the nurses who had been so helpful to me. It was better that way.

I would stay overnight, sleeping in the lounge. I could go to Ruth any time of the day or night. My face and voice became familiar to Ruth, and we bonded nicely. The nurses seemed surprised at first, but they got used to seeing me pop in at two in the morning.

The hospital held parenting classes for newborns in one of the lounges. I took advantage of them while I visited Ruth. They talked about everything: bathing, feeding, diapering, care of the umbilical cord, answering anything we wanted to talk about. It gave me more confidence as a mother.

Ruth was in her fourth week at the hospital. I think we were both growing weary of it all. Doctor Wilson would come in every so often, accompanied by a special pediatrician. He was the one who finally told me, "After all this time, we feel we can send Ruth home."

Home? I couldn't believe it. Doctor Wilson informed me that the spinal meningitis was clear, from a spinal tap that was taken over a week ago. They had done another one early that morning, and the results had come back still clear.

I had everything prepared at home. My mother's work place gave her a grandmother shower, and the gifts included blankets, shirts, booties, a swing, diapers, everything I could never have afforded on my own.

Even after Ruth got to leave the hospital, though, our weeks were filled with doctor visits. Doctor Wilson kept an eye on her kidneys and recommended other doctors who needed to be involved in Ruth's recovery. I was aware that at any time in her life, repercussions could result from her illness; retardation, cerebral palsy, learning disabilities.

Along with Doctor Wilson, Ruth had a neurologist, physical therapist, a pediatrician who specialized in children with birth difficulties, and blood work taken at the children's hospital every two months. Physical therapy was required, because after an initial test, Ruth seemed to lean to her left side. It was unknown if lack of oxygen to the brain or one of the other illnesses caused this reaction.

That first year of her life was filled with nothing but progress in her health. She defeated the odds and grew at a normal rate. She kept up as any normal baby would.

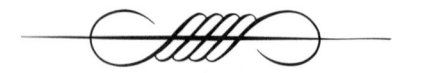

With my family's support, I didn't have to work. I stayed at my mother's house, cared for Ruth, and that was all that mattered. I was feeling better, also. My pregnancy had left me sixty pounds heavier, and my blonde hair had turned a dark brown.

During that first year, we were both recovering. I fit into my old jeans, colored my hair, and was able to deal with William's death better. My life was more positive with a new meaning. Soon I got an itching to have a job, make my own money, and live on my own with Ruth.

Some friends from highschool kept in touch. To go out and see a movie with a friend was a big deal for me. I felt out of touch with people my own age. I was involved with diapers and formulas, while they were dealing with college and work.

I needed to get out a little. My day to day life had become a routine, and time to myself was necessary. But I felt guilty if I wanted that. I needed to take a nap, or read a book, even just to sit back and listen to some of my favorite music. I found if you're not allowed that, you can lose all perspective. When I found time without my daughter, I was a better parent, a better, more-relaxed person.

I worked a couple of jobs, one after the other, and both were part time. It was good experience, and I struggled with balancing a job and caring for Ruth. A co-worker friend of my mother's had a small apartment over their garage. This was an opportunity for me to get out on my own.

My mother drove Ruth and me to see it. It was an A-frame shaped room, on top of the garage. We walked up the stairs and through the one and only door. Right away we were in the kitchen, the biggest part of the place. It had one bedroom, big enough for both Ruth and me, a small bathroom with washer and dryer attached, and the living room with a wood stove. It was interesting, with the high, peaked ceiling, and I felt it would suit us fine.

We moved in shortly after Ruth turned one. It was summer, and the warm days stayed trapped within our walls, even when the windows stayed open. My mother brought me over a huge fan. I was able to make ends meet, but it was always so close.

Every now and then my mother would help out with groceries, and I couldn't have asked for a cheaper monthly rent, but I wanted more for my life, especially with Ruth growing so quickly. I didn't want us to live there forever. I dreamed of a little house or condominium that I bought all by myself. I wanted to be able to support both of us without all the struggle and worrying.

I expressed my concerns to my mother. She told me of a job opening at her work. She didn't think I'd like it much, but I insisted she get me an application. I interviewed and got the job. It was full time, with benefits. My future was looking brighter, I told myself. My shift started at six a.m., Monday through Friday.

I didn't know it for quite a while, but my department was the same one William had worked in before he died a couple years earlier. My mom had given him a recommendation, and he had began working the night shift.

After two years, I was working around people who were some of the last to see him before his fatal auto accident. It was strange and oddly comforting.

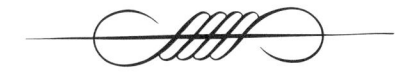

What was I going to do with Ruth? Thankfully a girlfriend of mine was available, but only for a short time. I had to think of getting a baby-sitter or a daycare. I was used to having my mother or my close friend take Ruth when I worked. I didn't want any-one else.

After that first day of work, I came home and saw my neighbor, who was also my landlady, working on some weeding. She looked to be a simple woman, with lightly browned skin, no makeup. Her black hair hung just above her shoulders. I didn't see her often, and didn't know much about her. I called to her, "Excuse me, Mrs. Simmons? Hi."

She was bent down struggling with an overgrown weed, but she looked up at me and smiled, "Hi there, how's everything going? Is the apartment ok? You're not having any problems with it, are you?"

"Oh no, I was wondering what you do with your son while you and Mr. Simmons are at work."

"Looking for a place for your daughter, huh? There's a daycare right across the street from Mr. Simmon's work. Well you also work there now, don't you? Oh, it would be perfect for you. It's a really nice place. It's in a house, set up for the daycare only, with a huge fenced backyard. I can give you the address, and you can stop by there, if you'd like. Mrs. Lawson, the provider, won't mind."

I was hesitant, "All right, yeah, I would like to check into it. I don't like to worry about Ruth while I'm gone.

"If I could find a place we both liked, it would be a huge weight off my shoulders."

Mrs. Simmons nodded, understanding. "Your daughter Ruth, right? She would get along well there. Lots of kids there are her age." I thanked her for the information and hurried up to my place to see Ruth and relieve my girlfriend of her duties.

The next morning I was up bright and early for work. I already was into it a week, and I could tell I wasn't much of a morning person. I think for the first two hours after I'm awake, I'm still in a light sleep, so it seems to make the morning go by fast. My job was not glamorous or really very interesting. I could see why my mother thought I probably wouldn't like the work.

My duty was to hang different shaped metal parts onto a pulley, then lower the parts into four or five different types of chemicals. The hot, smelly liquids cleaned and coated the parts before they moved on to their next step of assembly.

The people I worked with were very nice and seemed to keep to themselves. The majority of workers had been with the company for years and generally liked their job. But the smell of the chemicals left my stomach sick for some time, even after leaving the building, I wondered how the others could stand it.

The company had many different areas to work in. Each area had a particular duty, and I began to wonder if I could change mine. After only a few days, I wanted a new job. What a baby I am, I thought. But as I walked through the halls, I could see the other workers, and all the other jobs that were available, and I wanted one. I decided to wait as long as I could. Then I would apply for something different.

When the day shift was over, everyone made a beeline for the exit. It was quite a crowd. I usually stopped at a vending machine to purchase an apple on my way out. One day during my second week, a guy ahead of me took an apple, turned to me and took a bite of the fruit. I put my quarter in and pushed the button.

"An apple, huh? Good for you, but I swear you'd have to eat a whole tree of them if you want to get full." He looked into my eyes with a grin and left. What an odd guy, I thought. I shrugged it off and left for home.

Ruth and I went to visit the daycare. When we drove up, I was nervous. From the outside, it looked very well kept. It had a huge painted sign: "Rainbow Lane Daycare." I carried Ruth to the door with me. I could hear children playing inside, so I knocked loudly. A short woman answered the door. She had blond curly hair and wore thick glasses.

"Hi," I said, "Mrs. Lawson? Mrs. Simmons is a neighbor of mine. Actually I rent a room from her. Anyway, she said I should come and visit. I wanted to see if you had any room for my daughter."

The woman didn't smile, but she didn't look mean or angry either, "Simmons, yes. Her son Reagan is here. Come on in, and we can talk." I walked in and put Ruth down. Ruth stood there, soaking it all in. She had never been around so many kids at the same time. There were a couple of babies, one in a crib, and the other in a playpen.

The other children were older and played on the floor. Some played with blocks, others with stuffed animals and squeaky toys. Ruth saw two girls playing, who looked about her age. She walked over to them and stood, watching the two build with the colorful blocks, higher and higher until they fell over.

Ruth looked at me, as if to say, "Is it okay for me to play, too?"

"You want to play?" I asked walking toward her.

"Hi girls, this is Ruth. Ruth, sit down and let's see what happens." She sat, and the girls looked at each other, then at Ruth. They both offered her a block simultaneously. Ruth looked wary but accepted. I was so excited for her. Mrs. Lawson motioned me to the kitchen.

"Mrs. Simmons already told me that you might be stopping by. How old is Ruth?"

"She's about a year and a half," I replied.

Mrs. Lawson nodded, "I do have a opening for her age group. I care very much for the children who come here. The children are here, granted we all get along. That includes you and me." She seemed awfully stern I thought.

"When a child and I don't get along, it causes a lot of friction. I'm not going through a day all tensed up and stressed out if a kid and me clash."

I said, "Well I can understand that. It's not your job to straighten a child up. That's the parent's job."

"Exactly. So if you want to have Ruth here, it's on a trial basis first. Make sure she's comfortable and happy, and the same with me." That sounded fair, and although Mrs. Lawson was hard to read, she seemed to know what she was doing. My first impression was that she was sincere in caring for the children. Ruth was playing well, and Mrs. Lawson and I talked about her charges and other rules. Ruth would start tomorrow.

Things at work were going smoothly. My paychecks still weren't big enough, though. The company had a job posting board, and I had seen several openings. I signed up for one. It was in a different department, but just across the hall from the one I was at now. Even the pay scale was a little bit higher. So not even being at my position a month, I changed duties.

Now I worked with instrument circuit boards instead of bulky metal parts. And I still worked with chemicals, just not in liquid form. This department was mostly women, compared to the all-male station I was at before. It was nice to be around some females. I noticed the apple guy around a lot, leading me to believe he worked in the same area.

My lunch schedule was new also, and I spotted him there eating with a couple of other guys, laughing loudly and I could hear their off-color jokes. They seemed to be the obnoxious bunch of the building.

Everyone took a break at the same time. Most of the women would go outside to have a smoke. That left the majority of men behind. It was a little unnerving. I would get myself a snack and walk around or sit with a couple of the non-smoking women I knew. They all had worked with my mother at one time or another, before she had left to work at one of the new buildings.

"Mary, how's your mother doing?" asked Tina, a plump, dark-haired women who smoked like a chimney.

"She's doing good, thanks." I could remember some of these women from times my mother spoke of them. One had had a baby and another had gotten a promotion. It was weird to work with them, after all those years of hearing about them. They were always nice to me, but I felt like I didn't fit in much, so conversations were minimal.

It took me a while to get used to the men of the department. Their workspaces consisted of posters of half-naked women and bikini-clad girl calendars. They liked scoping out the single women who walked by. I wasn't used to being "hit on", for fun or not, so I'm sure I seemed offish, but I hadn't dated since Ruth's father had died.

The apple guy and I would run into each other in the hall or at break sometimes. He was short, with brown, shoulder-length hair. He always wore tight T-shirts and worn-out jeans, to accent his stocky build. He always made a smart-ass comment, not really rude, kind of funny. He seemed to be harmless to me and probably a nice guy.

I didn't find out much about him from my co-workers. There wasn't a lot of gossip. People made their own decisions about what they thought about everyone else. But I could tell who had been there the longest. They stuck by one another.

Most of the women had worked around each other for years. I knew my mother would know this guy, but I didn't want her opinion. I decided I shouldn't worry about it. I was too busy with Ruth and work. Anyway, I figured who wants to date a girl with a child?

Back at my station, a co-worker about my age, Erika, whispered to me, "His name is Rick." I looked at her, puzzled. "What? You mean the guy who's always eating an apple? How do you know?"

She smiled, "Cause I'm gutsy enough to ask. He doesn't have a girlfriend. Why don't you see if he'll go to a movie or something with you?"

I wasn't sure. "I don't know him or anything about him. I'm not comfortable doing that. Do you know anything else about him, other than the fact he doesn't have a girlfriend?"

Erika was working on cleaning a board, "No, I swear just because we're the new ones in this place, we don't get wind of any talk." Well, I thought to myself, Rick is his name. Maybe I'll try to talk to him, just get to know him better.

One Thursday afternoon we were informed we would be having a mandatory work day on Saturday, a five a.m. to eleven a.m. shift. After hearing that, I turned to whine to Erika about it, and there was Rick.

I smiled, "What are you doing out of your area? Escaped, did you?"

He gave me a smile back, "Yeah. Hey I was wondering, Saturday is a work day. Would you like to go to a late breakfast afterwards?"

I was shocked, and "Yes" popped out of my mouth without really thinking.

"Great," he said. "It's a restaurant in the area, just to let you know. Well, I'll see you later."

Erika had heard the quick conversation and looked surprised. Then a huge smile appeared on her face. I was unsure of my feelings, so I continued my work. I didn't want to discuss it.

When I got home I called my mom to see if she could take Ruth for that day. I told her of my required work morning and date. Date? That sounded weird to my own ears.

When she asked, "with who?" I was nervous. When I told her Rick, she couldn't believe it. I could hear shock and disappointment in her voice as she asked again, then again, "Rick?" She didn't give me a lecture, and she didn't need to. I was glad she hadn't tried to talk me out of it, because it made it easier to leave Ruth with her while I was gone.

Rick drove us to a restaurant not far from work. It was crowded, but the waitresses seemed to know Rick, with a big "hi" and a smile. We sat next to each other in a booth.

"I frequently eat here, it's got pretty good food, but I'll warn you, they pile it on your plate."

Through breakfast, I got to learn about Rick. He already knew that I had a child and my circumstances surrounding it. I had to remember, he had worked with my mom for quite a few years.

"So, how long have you worked for the company?" I asked.

He sighed, "Eight years, ever since I was eighteen. It's a long time to stay in one place, especially when you don't like the work."

I was curious, "Why don't you find something different? Even if it's in the same building, it seems there's a lot of positions you could apply for."

He shrugged, "I don't know what I want to do. I've gotten pretty comfortable where I'm at. I make okay money, so I figure why leave a good thing."

I was figuring, Why stay when you're miserable? I had also figured he was twenty-six to my twenty. Did I want to see a guy that much older than I? I found out he had a big family, two older brothers, two older sisters and one younger sister.

We had even attended the same private grade school, but with the age difference, he had been long gone by the time I started there. He liked to work out at the gym, and had even participated in some body-building contests.

Rick drove me back to the work parking lot where I had left my car.

"Thank you for breakfast, I said. It was nice to talk with you."

Rick nodded his head. "Yeah, maybe we could go and see a movie sometime."

I smiled, not sure what to say. "Well, see you later," and I shut his car door. I got in my car and sat there in silence for a while. I felt I shouldn't continue anything with Rick. It was nice to go out, but it felt too uncomfortable.

"Oh, don't be such a scaredy cat, go to a movie with him," Erika said Monday morning. "He seems to be a nice guy, and you haven't been out with a guy forever."

She was right; it was no big deal. It didn't have to become anything, maybe just a friendship. Erika and I were beginning to get reprimanded more times than not.

"You girls better start being quiet and putting out some production, said the department manager. You have plenty of time to talk on break or lunch."

She was right, but our job was so boring, I didn't have any interest in it at all. I knew I still hadn't found a job that I liked and felt that I was comfortable in. My grandmother likes to say, "That's just part of life. The majority of people don't like what they do, but it doesn't matter. A job is to make money, not to have fun or to be comfortable in."

I didn't want to live life with that attitude, and I certainly didn't want to live through life hating my job. I started to daydream of things that I liked to do. I liked to take pictures, so maybe I could be a photographer. I loved to write, so maybe I could put out a book. There had to be something I could do that I wanted to do. But I had to remember Ruth, and job fascination was risky.

Rick and I started to hang out with each other at breaks, and

I became more comfortable with him. We went to a movie one weekend and dinner the next. Things were building up slowly, and I started to think maybe this would be more than a friendship.

I recalled a time about two weeks before Ruth's dad was killed. We were talking, laughing about things that had happened in our day, but he suddenly became very serious. "If anything happens to me, I want you to find someone. I want you to find a guy you love, who will take care of you."

I had giggled, "What a thing to say. You're the one that's been designated to take care of me. Even if you want out, you're stuck."

He looked straight into my eyes, "I'm being serious, Mary. You'll have to go on, and I want to know that you'll find someone."

I hugged him, "Don't talk like that. I only want you, no matter what."

It made my stomach ill, but I had to wonder if Rick was that "someone." I told myself, "Just relax and go with things, keep an open mind. Try and keep things straight."

Rick had a motorcycle, and he wanted to take me for a ride. He wanted to make a day trip of it. Ruth's father had died riding a motorcycle, and I hadn't been on one since. But I had loved the speed, the rush of being out in the open air. After thinking about it, I accepted.

I took Ruth to my mother's early one Saturday morning. Rick said he would be by my place anytime. I dressed in my usual jeans, T-shirt and I put a sweater on over it for the ride. I heard the bike drive up. Its sound made my stomach flip. I can do this, I thought.

Rick stayed on the bike. He handed me a helmet and then I threw my leg over and got situated behind him. Oh, I was nervous, so I closed my eyes as we took off.

As I relaxed, I was brought back to the many rides I had had before, and all the memories rushed along with them. What were the chances that I would date a guy again with a bike? I wondered if it was a destiny thing. I had loved riding with William, and maybe this was some sort of sign. Rick and I rode through the hills and country, stopping for ice cream, then made our way back again. It had been a nice afternoon, nothing rushed, with no problems to think about. I decided maybe Rick had a place in my life after all.

I wanted to see where Rick lived, and I asked him if I could come over and make dinner for him sometime. He looked uncomfortable, "That's a great idea, but we should make it your place." I looked at him, hoping for an explanation.

"I'm at my parent's house right now, and it would be pretty awkward."

Immediately I thought he must have gotten himself into some financial problems. "Okay, Thursday night about five thirty." I said.

He looked away, thinking. "How about six-thirty? I'll be at the gym at five, so afterwards I'll come right to your place."

So it was a plan, I had decided to bake up something safe: potatoes, skinless chicken, and corn on the cob.

Rick arrived on time, and I was nervous for him to eat my meal. But he seemed to approve, and I was relieved. I thought it was weird that I felt so much pressure to impress him. Whatever the reason, I was glad when he had gone. I started to think about the fact that he lived with his parents. He probably rented a room, or maybe even part of the house like a basement.

He made pretty good money at work, so he probably had a good savings. There's nothing wrong with him or his situation, I told myself. It happens. But then I looked around my dinky apartment, all the struggles I have had. In the money area, still I was having problems. I thought maybe I should move back in with my family. No, that would make me feel like I was going backwards. I would make it all right so why couldn't he?

Rick and I had been seeing each other for four months. He had invited me to a movie for Friday night and asked me to meet him at his house. Was I going to meet his parents? I wasn't sure; he didn't say. Maybe they wouldn't be home. Maybe that was his plan, to invite me over if the folks aren't around.

I followed Rick's directions and found the house easily. I was greeted at the door by a woman, hair neatly pinned up and back, with glasses, and no makeup. She wore a simple sweatshirt and polyester pants. She smiled warmly, "Hello there, you must be Mary. Please come in, Rick will be ready anytime."

I smiled back at her and stepped inside. A gray-haired man sat in a recliner, reading the newspaper.

"Mary, my name is Claire, and this is Rick's father, Harold."

The man peered over his glasses at me, "Hello, there. Well, sit down, Rick's around here somewhere." Harold leaned over to take a sip of wine from a glass on the table. I noticed a cane leaned up against his chair.

"Rick, Mary's out here. Don't keep her waiting," he hollered.

The house was old, decorated modestly. The carpet was an old green color, and wood paneling covered the wall over the fireplace. Claire was busy in the kitchen doing the dishes.

"So Mary, where are you and Rick headed to tonight?" she said loudly. I stood up so I could see her.

"We're going to see a movie."

Rick came walking out of the hall. "Hi, you ready?"

"Sure," I said, "It was nice to meet you both, goodbye."

Rick put his arm around me, guiding me to the door. Outside, I commented, "Your parents seem nice." Rick didn't say anything. I thought maybe they had an argument. "So how long are you staying with them?"

Rick got the car started, "Well, they're retired now, so I'll be staying around while they do some traveling, you know, to keep an eye on things." I wanted to pursue the subject but decided it wasn't my business.

After the movie, Rick dropped me back off to my car at his house. He was tired and wanted to get to bed. That was fine with me; I had something on my mind. I was late with my period and didn't want to discuss it with him until I knew for sure.

The next morning I took a home pregnancy test, and it proved positive. I was a nervous wreck. All morning long I thought about what to say to Rick. Should I say anything at all? I was sure Rick didn't want any commitment, and this would definitely be one. I laid out all kinds of different scenarios in my mind as to what would happen when I told him. I decided it didn't matter what his reaction was. I would figure it out on my own.

Writing down monthly costs for a baby, compared to what I made it didn't add up. If Rick wouldn't help out, what would I do? My mother would be hugely disappointed, but I would ask for her help. The anxiety of thinking about it all morning was driving me crazy. I had to talk to Rick.

I phoned him, "Rick are you doing anything today?"

"No, you want to get together?"

"Well, I want to see you, I need to talk to you about some things."

"Sure, let's go to lunch, I know a great Mexican restaurant down by the beach. Come on over, and I'll drive us there."

I took Ruth to my mom's, even though she had just watched her the night before. I didn't normally go out two days back-to-back, so my mom was irritated.

"Could you please be back by three?" she asked. I have plans."

My mom had her own life and wasn't used to me depending on her so I could go out.

It was a warm sunny day. Rick and I ate our lunch out on the deck of the restaurant. I steered clear of what I really wanted to talk about, even though Rick asked numerous times, "What's wrong." I didn't want to talk about it while eating. In fact I had a hard time eating my taco salad, and Rick made note of it.

I asked if we could leave and drive somewhere quiet. We went down the street and parked on a hillside overlooking the beach. It was beautiful. I loved the beach. Usually it had a relaxing effect on me. But not today, my stomach was sick. Rick asked again, " What is on your mind?"

"Look, I'm just going to be blunt. I took a pregnancy test this morning, and I'm pregnant."

His mouth dropped slightly open. "Are you sure?" He laid his head back on the seat.

"Yes, I'm positive, and I don't expect anything from you, all right?"

He didn't say anything. He just started the car, and we went back. I didn't want to talk about it with him. By this time, I was getting angry at his reaction. I had figured there would be no joy or excitement from him on the news, but I guess I felt he'd at least talk with me about it.

I picked up Ruth and didn't stay to talk with my mom. I would tell her later. Monday at work, Rick stayed away from me all day, I didn't see him at break or lunch. I wasn't even sure if he was at work. It was like that all week. On Friday I went to where he was normally stationed, and he looked upset to see me.

"Hey, I'm just as shocked as you are, Rick, but you don't need to ignore me. I told you, well, because I didn't get pregnant all by myself and thought you should at least know. And what I said before, about not expecting anything from you, I mean that. We're not in love or anything like that, so do whatever you want."

I wanted to get it all out. "If you're having a problem dealing with it, we can talk about it, okay?"

He just nodded. "Look, work isn't the place to bring this stuff up. We'll talk later."

Great, I thought. He really was going to ditch me, now that I was pregnant. I felt horrible. Now I just had to find the right time to tell my family.

Rick continued to ignore me like the plague. People started to wonder what was going on. I was worried that the chemicals I worked with would affect the baby, so I talked to my supervisor about moving me. Then to my surprise I got a call from my mom at work. She was angry.

"Mary, I heard a rumor, and I hope it's a joke. Are you pregnant?"

My, how that got to her fast. And I thought the gossip around here was minimal. "Yes, I was going to tell you, I've only known for a couple of weeks."

"Did you tell him yet?"

"Yes, I told him and he isn't talking to me."

She calmed down, "I'm sorry; I just was shocked to hear it from someone other than you. Well, I'll help you any way you need it."

I was relieved to hear that. I felt better about things, and everyone around the building would know about it soon. Oh well, I said to myself, let them think what they want.

In my third month, Rick called me one evening and asked if he could come over. It was late, but I told him he could. When he arrived, he was in shorts and a tank. He had been at the gym.

"Mary," he began, "your being pregnant and all has been really a shock. It's taken me a long time to deal with it. I talked to my parents last night about it for the first time. After some time and discussing it with them, I've decided the best thing is to move in together. I'm partly to blame for all this, and I just want to do the right thing."

I didn't want his pity. "Rick, you can be a part of this if you want to, not because you feel you have to." He looked the other way, "I want to be; I've got responsibilities to account for, so I'll do it."

I didn't know what to think. How should I feel? I asked him to leave, because I was going to bed. I lay in bed, praying for direction, what was the best thing to do?

At work Rick and I would have lunch sometimes. It was never in the cafeteria; it was always somewhere in the remote part of the building.

Then he changed his lunchtime all together. He took a later lunch, which I was surprised he got. There were three lunches, divided according to departments. When I questioned him about it, he replied, "I just asked. Somebody must like me, huh?"

I was starting to show in my fourth month. Rick asked me to walk out to his car after work one day. We sat in the car, and Rick handed me a box. I opened it to find a heart-shaped diamond ring, I was totally surprised. And happy, because I thought it showed that Rick really did feel strongly about me, even though he had never said it. He stared out the window, "I was going to give it to you a little bit later on, but I figure I might as well do it now."

"It's really pretty, thank you."

I left his car thinking everything would work out, that this was the right thing, but as I drove to Ruth's daycare, I felt like a phony. I didn't really love Rick, so why was I feeling like I had to? I arrived at the daycare and showed everyone my ring. I acted like I was so happy, smiling and saying that Rick and I were going to find a place together.

Rick and I started looking for an apartment or a house with a reasonable rent. I would meet him at his house and we would look through the newspaper and go out to look at potentials.

Rick's parents were always at the house. It was uncomfortable for me to be there, especially as I got bigger. Claire was always pleasant, but Harold seemed angry. I suppose he was disappointed with the circumstances. I didn't blame him. I was disappointed, too, and deep down I was embarrassed and sad.

We finally found a place, a two-bedroom townhouse. Ruth would have to share a room with the baby, but it was affordable. It was clean and had lots of charm. I really liked it and couldn't wait to move in.

Ruth seemed to handle everything that was going on. I worried about the move, and Rick being in our lives and the baby coming, but Ruth seemed to be doing fine.

We were to move in at the end of the month and needed to sign the lease agreement. After work one day, Rick and I were to go and sign, but Rick said he couldn't make it, because he had plans and would do it later that day. So I went by myself and put down my signature, telling the owner Rick would be late. The next day at work, I didn't see Rick until lunch.

"Did you make it all right to the apartment to sign the papers?" I asked hopefully.

Rick sat down "I want to talk to you about that. I was figuring some things out last night. When you have the baby, you're going to want to take some time off, right? You won't be having any money coming in, and I don't think I can handle the rent by myself while you're not working."

"I don't understand," I said. "We had this all worked out that if we got a place with a good rent, we could handle it for three or four months with me not working. Any money I'm making right now I'm saving the best I can, to go for rent during that time."

He looked nervous, "All right, I know we've discussed this before, and it all seemed fine, but with the baby, it's going to take a lot of money to support it, and I can't do it alone financially."

I was disappointed. He was backing out of it all, and I was in my eighth month.

"Look," he said, "my parents are leaving soon and said you and Ruth could move in while they're gone. After the baby you can take some time off, and I won't have to worry about money so much. I'll be making the mortgage payments while they are gone, and that's no big deal. They've had that house for so long, it's under two hundred a month. This is the only way, Mary."

I asked him if we could give the apartment a chance. I didn't want to live in his parent's home. He refused. I told him I had to think about it.

I sat at my place, thinking about what Rick had said. I had been in my apartment for about a year, and Ruth and I were growing out of it. We had our problems: mildew in a back closet, and mice visiting at night. The place was freezing in the winter and too hot during the summer. And sharing a room with Ruth; well, Ruth was getting too big for that. She needed her own bed, instead of a crib and dresser and shelves for her dolls.

I wanted to ask my mom if Ruth and I could move back in with her and stay for a while after I had the baby. That sounded good to me. It was time that I started being honest with myself about Rick.

If Rick wasn't in my life, I figured it didn't matter. I didn't feel any kind of sadness. If he wanted to be in the baby's life, great. I know Ruth would have benefitted greatly if her father had been around. But I thought about my mom. She had her place all to herself, since my brother had recently moved out. It was a new life for my mom. I couldn't ask her. I would feel guilty.

I decided I would move into Ricks house. His parents wouldn't be there, and it would only be for a while, until I got back to work again. I would just have to do it. I felt I had no other choice.

Claire and Harold didn't leave until I was well into my ninth month. Harold had made it clear that with my moving in, Rick and I had to have separate bedrooms. Rick abided by the rule and kept his usual room, located next to his parents. There were three bedrooms upstairs: Rick's, his parents', and the third was a storage place. It had boxes and clothes in it. There was a room in the basement.

"Rick, where are the kids going to sleep?" I asked one night.

"I didn't think of that," he said. "Well, they can use my room, and I'll clean out the storage room for me."

So we set up a crib, and I bought new sheets for Rick's bed that Ruth would be using. I decorated it with all the things she enjoyed. When it came time for her to sleep in the room, though, she hated it.

"I don't want to stay in here," she said. This is not my bed, it's Rick's."

We went through this every night. I stayed with her till she fell asleep, but she would be up again later in the night. I was already exhausted from carrying the baby, so Ruth's problem turned me into a zombie. She would end up sleeping with me most nights. I knew she was uncomfortable.

Rick hadn't cleaned up the third room, so he was sleeping on the couch. While I waited to give birth, I cleaned and did laundry.

It was odd for me; I had never been responsible for anyone else but Ruth and me. To do things for Rick, I felt like I was a wife or a maid.

With the budget Rick gave me, I prepared meals the best I could: chicken, potatoes, frozen veggies, soups, sandwiches, whatever I could think of. Rick was getting sick of it by the third week of our living together. He complained he missed the big meals his mom would cook, like pot roasts, and casseroles. I was frustrated. He made me feel I was a failure, but I figured I should be grateful, right? He and his family were doing me a favor, allowing us to live in their home.

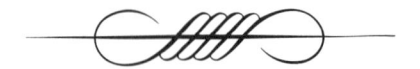

One Saturday morning my mom came to get Ruth to spend the day together, to give me a chance to rest. Rick mowed the lawn and I did some housework. That afternoon, I was feeling the contractions. I dealt with them pretty well, not knowing if they were false or not. I started dinner, a meal with noodles, meat and a gravy. Maybe that would impress Rick.

He took a nap on the couch while I cooked. I decided to call my doctor, since the contractions seemed continuous. She told me to meet her at the hospital. I called my mom to let her know what was going on. I woke Rick, telling him it was time to go to the hospital. He looked grumpy, "All right, I'll go start the car. You got your bag ready?"

I did, and we started off to the hospital. The pain really kicked in, halfway there. Every bump we hit, I felt right in my abdomen. We arrived, finding that I was already five centimeters dilated. I was so proud of myself; I really hung in there. Rick filled out medical papers for me. The labor was in high gear now.

Within the next fifteen minutes I was crying for relief, "Give me some pain killers!" The nurse, seeing me lose control, sternly said, "You're almost there, you're going to do this naturally, there's no time for a shot. You need to calm down, you're scaring the other patients, do you understand?"

With those words she whipped me out of my frenzy, and I began to concentrate on getting the baby out.

My doctor arrived, and within one hour I had a nine pound baby boy. Born eight fifty five p.m, March 19, 1988. Rick had come in at the last part, to tell me to push. I needed all the support I could get. The baby, Jack, had swallowed some fluid, but the great nurses and doctor had called for help, and said he would be fine.

I felt great after having Jack. Rick had fallen asleep in a chair in my room. My mom and Ruth came to visit. I was glad it was over. The nurses needed to move me to another room, telling Rick they would bring him some blankets and pillows, and he could sleep in the lounge.

"I think I'll go home," he said. "I'll come back tomorrow." And he left.

I got comfortable in my new bed, and a nurse brought me my huge baby boy. I fed him, and he slept with me. He was doing great, so the nurses left him in my room as much as possible. Rick came by Sunday morning. He sat there, looking like he had just woken up.

"Did you put the meat in the refrigerator for me?" I asked. "It was too hot to put away last night when we left."

He nodded and stood up, "I'm going to get going; I've got some things to do, but I'll come back tonight."

"The doctor said Jack and I can leave tomorrow morning. Can you pick us up?"

"Yeah, I took a week off of work. I'll be here."

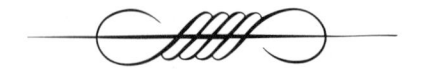

Throughout the day I had visitors, and I was happy, I sensed Rick was having a problem but I didn't let it bother me. Later in the evening I expected to see Rick, but I got a call instead.

"Hi, Mary? Its Jane. I'm calling because Rick wanted me to tell you he's over here watching a basketball game with Dean."

"How come he didn't call me?"

"Well he's pretty drunk."

"I want to talk to him, please."

"Hello?" Rick slurred, "Mary, I'm not going to be there ok? I'm watching a once-in-a-lifetime game. But I'll be there tomorrow morning."

"Whatever, Rick. We'll be ready by nine."

Jane got back on the phone, "I'm sorry Mary; I told him he should be with you, but he wouldn't go."

It wasn't her fault. Rick had the choice of how he wanted to deal with the situation. I would like to have seen him have the baby! Would he leave it to go watch a game and have a few beers afterwards?

The next day, as soon as we arrived back at the house, a gloom set over me. I was not happy where I was. I wanted to leave at that moment. The house was a mess. My dinner was still on the stove, the meat ruined.

Newspapers were strewn all over the kitchen table and on the floor. Dishes and glasses lay in the sink, not even soaked, encrusted with food.

I had only been gone a day and a half. I got out the vacuum and cleaned the floor, did the dishes, and threw in some laundry. I was upset, and I was seeing a picture now, of why Rick lived at home. They were none of the reasons I developed in my head. He was a baby himself. He needed someone to take care of him, and his parents allowed that. That's why I was here.

I would get out of here as soon as I went back to work in three months. No, I'd have to ask my mom for help. I couldn't stand living here with Rick. I was mad at myself for all sorts of things: letting things slide, not voicing my opinions. I was seeing the real Rick and finally seeing the real me.

The week Rick went back to work, his schedule changed. He would be working the three p.m to midnight shift. While he was getting ready to leave for his first day back I asked, "Why are you working that shift? Someone sick?"

Rick went to get his coat,"Well, I volunteered. They're down a couple people and asked any of us daytime people if we wanted a change to work nights. I used to work that shift a few years back, I like it; the time goes by fast."

And he left. Rick had moved into the room in the basement. He slept most of the day, getting up only to watch cartoons and eat something.

Most of the time the kids and I were gone. Ruth was involved in a preschool class at the daycare, so she went just about every day from nine till noon. Jack and I would get her there, and maybe go visit my mother at work, or my grandmother at her home. Sometimes we'd just go out for a drive.

About noon one day, Rick appeared from the basement. I was surprised, "Hi, Rick, we're not used to seeing you up so early."

He smirked, "Well, I've been noticing when I leave for work you guys aren't around. How come?"

Did he really care? "I get tired of being here all the time. We don't see much of you, so we go out, anywhere."

Rick stood there for a moment like he didn't understand what I was saying, then made his way to the bathroom to take a shower.

Two months passed. I hated being alone at night. I'd hear a creak, and I was up. I found myself checking around the house and then falling asleep on the couch. The garage door didn't lock, which meant that anyone could come in and climb the stairs to the house. I asked Rick if he could install a lock either on the garage or the door for protection.

"Mary, I've lived here all my life, and we've never had any problems. This is a safe neighborhood."

"That's the problem Rick, you get so comfortable about things not being locked up, someone not so nice is going to notice. And why have you lived here all your life?"

I had stunned him; I had never come out so bluntly with that question. He walked away from me like a wounded animal. I went and bought a door lock, but couldn't get it to work. Rick said he would do it if it bothered me so much, but he never did.

Thirteen weeks after I had Jack, I was starting to feel like I was losing energy. I told myself that because of the new baby, I was tired. Jack woke up about three one morning, crying. I got up to get his bottle, and I dropped to the floor, sitting in my own blood. I didn't hurt anywhere, but I felt dizzy and just sat still.

Rick's room was right below mine, so I pounded on the floor with my fist, then my heel. I waited to hear him come through the house, but nothing happened. Jack continued to cry, I made it to the bathroom where I wrapped myself up in a towel. I got his milk, and he drank it and fell back to sleep. I went back into bed and waited for daylight. I called my doctor, and she couldn't tell me what was wrong, "Sounds like a heavy period Mary. Your first one since the baby?"

It was, but it wasn't just a heavy period. It left me so weak.

"Keep your feet up, she suggested. No housework, no picking up the kids, just rest. Call me if it gets worse."

I explained to Rick my problem and asked for his help. "It's the weekend," I said. "And if I rest I'm sure I'll be fine by Monday."

He reluctantly took the kids to a get-together his family was having. When they arrived back at the house, I asked, "How did it go?"

"Fine," he said.

"Did anyone ask why I wasn't there?" I wanted to know, I liked chatting with a couple of his sisters and hoped they understood why I wasn't there.

"Not really, I just said you were sick. With some female problems."

I was offended. He really thought I was boo-hooing about some "female problems"? His lack of concern was disheartening.

Sunday evening I felt so bad, Rick had to drive me to the emergency room per my doctor's order. After an examination and some blood samples, the doctor felt I wasn't finished with my healing and some hemorrhaging had occurred. I was told right in front of Rick to do nothing but rest. I was to start back to work the next week, and the doctor was worried because I would be on my feet all day. I told her I would rest up before then.

I asked Rick to move back upstairs. He did. But instead of fixing up the third room, he made his bed in the den, on the other side of the house. That week Rick acted as though nothing was wrong. His parents had been back for about two weeks, staying in their trailer parked beside the house, and he told them I was fine. So I was uncomfortable asking for their help, so I just worked with it, getting to bed early, and taking a variety of vitamins.

The weekend before I started back to work, Rick came to me with a suggestion. "My parents want to watch Jack while you start back to work. He's only three months old and a daycare will be too much for him, you know other kids, picking up their germs, colds. So while they're here, let's let them take him during the day."

I was opposed. "I want to take him with his sister, and I don't want to rely on your parents. They're retired, so they should be doing other things, not spending their day watching the baby."

"Well, I want to do it, it will save me a lot of money."

That seemed to be the magical argument, money, so I agreed. They would be here for another three months, and when Jack was six months old, he would go to daycare with Ruth.

Going back to work was rough. I was still bleeding heavily, even having to go home to change. It lasted another three weeks. Rick left for work before me and got back after I was home. Claire came to the house each morning at six, always on time. I took Ruth to the daycare and picked her up immediately after work.

When we got back to the house, it was usually Harold taking care of Jack. Harold had suffered from polio when he was younger, and I worried that he would drop the baby. Rick told me not to worry, "My father has done anything he wants to. Polio can't stand in his way."

"I understand that. It's great he has dealt with it in that manner, but we're talking about an infant. If your father is carrying him and he loses his balance, then what?" I argued.

Rick shrugged, "We'll deal with that when and if it happens."

I knew Claire missed having her home. When I was at work she would do laundry, cook up some homemade jam or soup, use the bathtub, weed the yard, or just read a book in one of the recliners. Everything in the house was just how they left it when I moved in. I didn't bring any of my stuff to their home. I felt like an intruder and was determined to get out on my own.

I didn't think about if Rick would be with us or not. We didn't have a relationship. We never talked, never went out together expect for a reunion for his wrestling class from high-school, and I felt he would never leave home. Claire always did his wash, made his bed, and cleaned his room. I would never do it, so she did. I had worked only one month at my job when one of Rick's sisters told me about a cashier position at a grocery store. But the hours were mainly nights and weekends, and I didn't want that.

Then she suggested I apply at another store that needed a part time bookkeeper. I had little experience, but went and interviewed and got the job. It had great benefits, good pay, and the hours were morning to afternoon. I knew I would need full time if I were to get out on my own again, and hoped I could use the experience to achieve that. I was feeling pretty good and had started to lose the weight gain from being pregnant.

Harold and Claire continued to watch Jack through the summer time. On my weekdays off, I took the kids to the park or to the beach. Ruth loved playing in the sand, and Jack would watch the seagulls from his carrier. Sometimes Ruth would go to daycare for the playtime with her friends. It gave Jack and me a chance to have one-on-one time together.

Rick had decided to change jobs. Through one of his other sisters, he studied to be an electrician. He started school, going every Tuesday night. He had to study, so Saturday or Sunday, a friend of his would help him understand the math that Rick needed to know. They spent most of the day, sometimes the evening, doing this.

Rick helped out with a diaper change here and a bath there,

I showed him the proper ways, and he got more comfortable as Jack got bigger. I was glad he took some interest in Jack. Summer was ending, and, with autumn approaching, Harold and Claire wanted to get back to the warm weather of Arizona. Jack was just about six months old and I was excited to be able to take both of the kids together to daycare. Ruth had been asking why Jack didn't go with her. "Why does he stay behind?" she asked me.

I told Rick, "Your parents are making plans to travel again, right? It was really nice of them to take care of Jack while they were here. I want to start Jack at the daycare next week."

"Let's talk about that." Rick said. "There's this lady at the end of the cul-de-sac that has a daycare, and I think Jack should go there. She's a friend of my sister, and we've known her for a long time. She only has a couple of kids, and it would be better for Jack not to be exposed to a house full of kids and babies."

I was surprised, "How long have you been thinking of that? We already discussed that when your parents left, Jack would go with Ruth. I don't want to split them up anymore."

"My dad talked to me about it and said she doesn't charge as much, and that would help. She'd be real good with Jack."

I was annoyed, "Just because your dad says we should do that doesn't mean it will happen. Your dad tells you I can move in here, so I do, your dad wants he and your mother to watch Jack for a few months, so they do, and now this. How about we discuss things and do what we think is best for the kids." I said.

Rick wouldn't agree, "How about Jack goes to this gal until he is a little bit older? Then we can talk about the daycare. Ruth didn't start daycare until she was about a year old, right?" I let it happen.

I visited the woman up the street, Kelley. She seemed nice, and had two children of her own. I signed some papers. Jack would start there the following Monday morning. I was sad to leave him there, and to take Ruth without him. Harold and Claire left two weeks later.

I was glad they were gone. I had felt I was under a microscope with Harold. He would tell me how to feed Jack, what he should wear. I grew to feel uncomfortable around him and wondered if Rick felt that way also. Rick seem to comply with Harold's "suggestions". Maybe that was a great factor in why Rick remained at home. I was told by my mother that Rick once dated another girl from our previous workplace. They dated for about two years, and Rick wanted to marry her. What a shocker. Rick picked living at home over living with a woman he loved. Why didn't it happen?

Jack went to Kelley's for the next two months. Then she and her family would be gone for two weeks on a holiday vacation. Where would Jack go? I suggested the daycare. So for two weeks Jack and Ruth attended together while I worked. Jack loved it. There was another little boy his age, and they would sit together playing blocks with eachother. Ruth was proud to have her little brother there with her.

I told Rick about all the things the kids were doing. I told him how much Jack liked going. "This will be the best for the kids," I said "to stop separating them. Having them together is much less worrisome for me." Without his parents around, he didn't have any argument, and sent Kelley a note letting her know and thanked her for her help.

By the time Jack turned one, I was still working part time. I had learned quite a bit from the head bookkeeper I worked with, she talked about wanting to leave the company. I told her that if she did, I wanted a chance at her job, and opened up to her with the reasons why.

Harold and Claire came back into town that next spring. Harold seemed very shocked when we told him Jack was going to the daycare. He asked Rick if he could talk to him privately. I don't know what was discussed.

Jack was still having problems at night. He would get up crying until he got a bottle, then wouldn't drink much. He wouldn't take a pacifier. I took him in to the pediatrician for his one-year checkup. The doctor reiterated what I already knew, "Let him cry it out, as long as he doesn't get out of hand. When you put him in for a nap or bedtime, let him cry then. He's gotten himself into a bad habit. At night he doesn't get up and cry because he's hungry. He's just used to it."

I told Rick about our doctor visit. That night I got the kids to bed. Jack fussed and cried. I went in, "It's all right, you're okay." I hugged him and left. I sat out in the living room listening to him, making sure he didn't get too upset.

Rick came storming out of the den. "What is going on? I'm trying to watch a movie, and I can't hear a damn thing with all that crying. Why aren't you handling it?"

I stood up,"Because I already told you why; I told you what the doctor said."

Rick came down the hallway with Jack. "Well, I don't remember him being like this."

"That's because I always gave him a bottle or carried him around until he fell asleep. You always want quiet at bedtime, but I've never given him the chance to get to sleep by himself," I said.

Rick went back to the den and watched his movie, rocking Jack until he was asleep.

Summer had arrived again so quickly. Jack was ready for his first haircut. "Rick" I said, "you want to take Jack to the barber's?"

Rick smiled, "I guess so. You think he needs one?"

"Yes, I had a lady at the store the other day tell me what a cute little girl he was. Ruth and I will do some girl stuff together. I think she would like that."

So Jack came back with his hair cropped to his little neck,

Rick got a shave also. After that Rick felt more comfortable about taking Jack places with him. They would go mostly to one of Rick's friend house, Dean, who was recently divorced and had a daughter who was just a little older then Jack. Jane had left, and from what I understood, not wanting the parenting responsibility any more.

During the summer, Harold and Claire did their own thing. Harold would ask if he could take Jack instead of letting him go to "that daycare place". I always refused, trying to show him we didn't need to rely on him. I invited Claire and Harold for a Sunday dinner. I made a ham with potatoes and vegetables. At the table, we talked about how the kids were doing, and I mentioned that Jack was using his cup so well, he'd be off his bottle soon.

Harold didn't like that. Looking directly at Rick he said, "He is still a baby; don't force him off the bottle." Rick didn't reply so I did.

"He's over a year now. That bottle is a reason he gets up at night. He's old enough to take a cup."

Harold persisted, "He is too young. That bottle gives him all he needs."

I obviously was not going to be heard. I worried about having Rick's parents around again. Harold kept going to Rick with his opinions, and then Rick was to come to me. I hated that game. Fall came, and finally Harold and Claire left again.

At work there were a lot of people my age and I made some new friends. There was talk again that there might be a full time position for me soon. I couldn't wait. Rick and I had the house again, and I wanted to be out by the time Harold and Claire arrived back in spring.

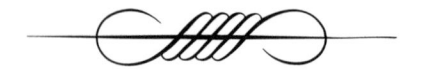

For Jack's second birthday party, we had the whole family over, Rick's as well as mine. It went smoothly, and Jack had a great time. After everyone had left, one of Rick's older sisters stayed behind. They talked in the kitchen, and I caught some of their words.

"Rick, you and Mary need to get out of the house. Mom would really like to either sell or rent it out. She and dad are talking about buying some land in Arizona, and they can't do it with you guys here."

"I can stay here as long as I want. Dad said so," Rick said.

His sister persisted, "You're making really good money as an electrician, so you can't tell me that you and Mary can't make it on your own. Will you just think about what I've said? It would mean a lot to mom to be able to worry about herself instead of you and Mary."

I felt awful. After she left, I confronted Rick, "I didn't mean to eavesdrop, but I heard what you two were talking about. She's right. We've been here for two years. The time has flown by, and we never did what we said, that we would stay for just a while until I was working again."

"Don't worry about her. I don't have to listen to any of them. My dad said I can be here as long as I like."

"What do you mean "any of them"? Has someone else talked to you about it?"

"My brothers and sisters. But I'm not listening."

The weekend had come. It was Sunday. We all usually went to Mass together but I didn't want to. I was depressed about our living situation, about living with Rick and no relationship, and I was searching for a solution. "I'm taking Jack with me to church," Rick said after I let him know I was staying home.

I did some laundry. I called my mom to see if she was home. I wanted to go over there to talk to her about everything. I figured I would swallow my pride and ask for her help. Ruth and I left with the washer and dryer going. After being at my mom's for about forty-five minutes Rick called. "Mary, there's been a fire at the house! It started in the den and the whole house is ruined."

I went back right away. It was a mess. The den was charred as well as everything in it. All the kid's toys, furniture, clothes, a TV. From one end of the house to the other, the smoke had left its mark. The smell was sickening. Rick was on the phone.

"I can't believe it," I said. Where's Jack?"

Rick could hardly talk, "Across the street."

I went over and thanked the neighbor for watching him, "Would you mind if he and Ruth stay here a little longer until I talk to Rick more about all this?"

She didn't mind. She was a nice neighbor. We had talked a few times before.

I went back to the house, and Rick was sitting in shock in the living room, "There's nothing we can do, being that it's Sunday." He said. "I'll call the insurance company tomorrow. Hopefully my parents will call soon." The house was cold. Some of the windows had blown out.

"We can stay at my mom's." I said. "I'll go get Jack and Ruth; you meet us there when you want."

But Rick stayed at the house for a long time. He waited to hear from Harold. Later he arrived saying his parents would leave immediately to get back.

Rick talked with the insurance people and they started right away surveying the damage. Harold and Claire arrived within three days.

"Claire I am so sorry this happened. "I said.

She smiled "As long as no one was hurt, it will be fine, this all can be fixed. You and Rick should look for a hotel or apartment, something inexpensive. The insurance will cover a place for you guys to stay while things are being fixed."

Great, I thought, It was pretty crowded with us all at my mom's. I told Rick. "Well, you start looking in the paper then," he said, "because I'm going to be busy helping my dad with all this." So I did. I didn't take any work off, but Rick took some time off to help with his folks. He was keeping Jack during the day, and I knew it was because of Harold.

After work, Ruth and I went to the house, no one was there. I didn't know where to find anyone. I went back to my mom's hoping Rick would call to tell me what was going on. He called "Mary? I'm over at Dean's. I think we're going to stay here tonight."

"Rick, why Dean's? Come back over here or at least bring Jack over."

"It'll be fun, just the boys; I'll bring Jack to the daycare in the morning. I'm going back to work."

"Well. okay, but we need to sit down and figure out a place to stay. The insurance will cover it, and I think we should do it."

When I dropped Ruth off at daycare, I saw Jack was already there. I gave him a hug, and when he saw Ruth he ran to give her a squeeze . When I went to get the kids later that day, Jack wasn't there. "Did Rick already pick up Jack?" I asked one of the girls.

"No, Grandpa did."

What nerve I thought. I went to the house but the only ones there were the insurance people. Rick called me later at my mom's.

"Jack and I are at Dean's; we're going to hang out here."

"Rick, your dad picked up Jack at the daycare, and I didn't know anything about it. I'm coming over to Dean's right now. We need to talk."

I went inside the house and picked up Jack. "Rick, I don't want Jack to stay here. I want to get a place, why do you ignore that subject?" Rick looked down, "Because it's not going to happen. The insurance policy is for my parents. They're covered, not us. And they have their trailer, so they don't need a place to stay while the house is being fixed."

"Why hasn't anyone told me? Here I'm thinking for two weeks now, we're getting a place. Well, would Dean mind if we rented a couple rooms from him?"

" There's not enough room for all four of us," he said. "Jack and I can stay."

"I don't want Jack staying without me. Come back to my mom's then."

"No, your mom's place is too crowded. How about you and Ruth stay there, and Jack and I will stay here? It won't be for too long. I'll see if my folks can help us get a place. Anyway it will be fun for Jack and me, kind of a guy thing."

For whatever reason, I complied, "You guys can sleep here, but I want to see Jack every day until his bedtime." Rick smiled and nodded his okay.

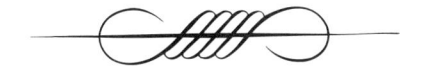

I started working full time, and my mom helped me find an apartment. Rick and I would not be getting back together. I saw Jack every day, and my kids spent time together during the day until bedtime. I hated the arrangement, but I felt helpless with so little money. As soon as I found an affordable place to live, Rick's parentshouse was finished. All new carpeting, they knocked a wall out that separated the den and living room, new wallpaper and paint. Everything looked very up-to-date.

Harold and Claire got a new house, so to speak, because of the fire, which happened because the dryer's heat valve had been set too high. Rick moved right back in. "How come you're living there again? I asked. "Aren't you going to get a place for yourself?"

"Yeah, after I save some money, I'll be out of here." Save some money? He made fifteen dollars an hour, so what was he doing with it?

I continued, "Well we need a schedule for Jack." And over the phone I told Rick what I thought would work. I took into consideration his school night and study day, and there were two weekdays that I worked that were longer than the others. Rick agreed with the schedule.

There were problems, though. Rick's parents were gone again, and he seemed to have a difficult time with Jack.

We were potty training Jack, but Rick still used diapers. When Rick dropped Jack off at the daycare, they noted that Jack was dirty and tired, falling asleep sometimes while having lunch. He would wet his pants several times, because when he headed for the toilet, he walked so slowly.

Then after about four months, Harold and Claire were back in the picture. Jack wasn't at the daycare on Rick's days. I could see it wasn't going to work. Jack was having trouble going to Rick's, then mine, not being at the daycare, having his grandparents take care of him. He seemed so confused. The only thing I could think of was that I needed to talk with a lawyer to see what I should do. So from a family recommendation, I went to visit Mr. Chan.

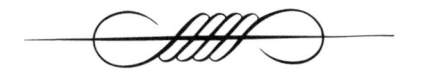

"Mr. Chan, I have two children from two separate relationships." I continued to tell him my story. "What do I need to do?" I asked.

"You need a parenting plan," he said. "I can write one up for you according to the law, and you sign it and we send it off to Rick, and you get on with your life. Mary, you're a good mother. It sounds like you've had some tough times. You want the father in your son's life, and you want a schedule that will be healthy to your son.

"Most women just want to write the father off when things go bad. And he hasn't even claimed legal paternity, and the kid is almost three? What does that say? He wants to be a part of the child's life, but he's not willing to go as far as to make it legal? Mary, if it went to court, no judge in his right mind would go against you."

"Court? I don't want to go to court. I want just want something legal, a parenting plan you said? Yeah, that's what I want. How much would that cost?"

Mr. Chan leaned back in his chair, "It would be fairly simple; it has a lot to it, but I could write it up, get it notarized and have it served to him for seven hundred dollars." I didn't have that. "Well, I'll start saving," I said, "and I'll get back to you later."

Within a couple of months, I raised the money and visited Mr. Chan again. We discussed holiday and special-day visitation. We talked about child support and got a rough estimation of what Rick would pay each month. "Mr. Chan, I don't think five hundred is reasonable. It doesn't take that much to support Jack. Can we lower it a few hundred?" I asked.

Mr. Chan looked up from his writing, surprised, his glasses bright from the lamp on his desk. "No, that's the state's deal. I take in consideration what you make, what Rick makes; I get a percentage of what the both of you are responsible for, and I take it to a child support table, much like a tax table, and get an actual money amount."

After we finished, I gave him his fee.

"Thank you, Mary. When I'm all finished, I'll give you a call and let you know when he'll be served."

Two weeks later I got that call. I was nervous,

"Mr. Chan, what time will he be getting it?"

"Some time after three. All he has to do is sign it and get it back to me within ten days. I wouldn't let Jack visit Rick until this is settled. Wait until everything is done and made legal."

Keep Jack from Rick? I couldn't see that going over too well.

I tried to get the kids down for a nap. I told them they could sleep out in the living room while I did some laundry. Ruth and Jack went and found all the blankets and pillows they could and dragged them out. Piling them upon each other, a cozy bed was made. The kids got comfortable, and I picked a book to read. Ruth asked if she could read it. She was in first grade now, and wanted to show us her reading skills.

She did well. Even the words she didn't know, she made up according to the picture. Jack marveled at her performance. His eyes went from the book to her mouth. The phone rang. It was Rick.

"Mary, I got this crap you sent me," he said. "Who do you think you are? You're not going to screw with me."

I could feel my face get hot, "I'm not 'screwing' with you. Something needs to be done for Jack. It's a schedule, did you look at it?"

His voice grew louder, "Yeah, I looked at it, and you're screwing with the wrong person. You think you can just mess me over? I'm not going with your plan, you're not getting your way."

"Rick I'm not messing with you over or anything. I just want Jack to feel stable. Read through the papers and calm down and you'll see." I was hesitant on my next sentence, "My lawyer says you shouldn't see Jack until all this is cleared up."

Rick was screaming "Screw you! I'm going to get you okay? Hey you want Jack so bad? I'm gonna make it harder than hell for you then. You want a custody battle? That's what I'll do. I'll give you a battle you'll regret." He laughed, "See ya in court, you bitch!"

He hung up. My hands were freezing. He really got me scared. I had never heard so many swear words come from his mouth so many times at once in a conversation. Did he really believe it was a power trip I was on? I would have to wait the next ten days out and see.

The next week was rough. I expected Rick to come to my apartment in a rage, but he didn't. He found himself an attorney. My attorney was served notice that we were going to court over it. Just like that, my simple parenting plan was now a custody case. Rick made himself and my son the plaintiffs and I the respondent. I called Mr. Chan, "What should I do? I don't want to go to court. Tell me what's going on, please."

Mr. Chan sighed, "Well, Rick wants custody, and he found a lawyer that will help him. I just don't see it as a big problem Mary. He's an ex-boyfriend, he still lives at home, you are a good mom, you've got another child in the picture, Jack's sister, half-sibling or not. You're not unfit in any category, so I wouldn't worry, if I were you."

But I did, "I don't have the money to get me through a court battle. How long do you think it will take?"

Mr. Chan replied,"I'm sure Rick's attorney will pull some crap, try and drag unnecessary things out. I'd say a couple of months, and probably two days in court."

Two weeks went by and I was served with papers ordering me to appear for an oral deposition. My boyfriend, Mike, was served as well. He had been living with the kids and me for a couple of months now. I had met him while working at the grocery store. He was a manager, and being the same age, we had become friends.

At the time we met, Mike had a girlfriend, and I was living with Rick. But after my move and Mike's girlfriend was gone, we started dating.

We met at my lawyer's office and I met Rick's attorney, Mr. Hooper, for the first time. He smiled, shook hands as if he were a very pleasant man. But an oral deposition is nothing more then a grill session. A court reporter types the questions and answers, so hopefully it can be used against you when court time comes around. Mr. Hooper was very snide. I broke into tears when he questioned me about Ruth and the situation with her father. He liked it.

He called for a break, and everyone got up, but I wanted to continue. He turned to me and smiled brightly, "Oh, no, we'll break now," and he began to talk to Rick in soft tones. After Mike and I were finished with the questioning, Mr. Hooper brought up the schedule for Jack. "We want it fifty-fifty until it gets to court. My client has every right to his son. He has admitted paternity, and we want the relationship to continue between a father and his son."

I didn't agree; it would be bouncing Jack here and there. Mr. Chan whispered to me, "Agree, we'll be in court soon, and if we show what happened here today and how you complied with a temporary plan, I can show the judge you don't disagree with the father's rights, and that you are a willing and considerate mother."

So I signed. Mike and I went into Mr. Chan's office. "It went well. They didn't get any juicy things out of you that they can use. It's a simple case. You don't have anything to worry about."

Because of my son's age, three and a half, we needed to agree on a guardian ad-litem who would represent Jack in court. This person needed to be qualified and unbiased. We came to a mutual decision on a woman attorney to be the eyes and ears for the judge. Mr. Hooper also suggested we have a court-appointed family investigator. He didn't want to leave any stone unturned.

Within the next few months, these two experts did their investigation. The family investigator was paid for by the state, but Rick and I split the payment on the guardian, which was quite hefty. The two women's responsibilities were to visit the daycare, scheduled or not, talk with the providers, visit us at home, and do any type of research that would help them determine the best thing for Jack. The guardian would visit Rick's home first. He made an odd request. "Come and talk with my parents first, and then me."

The guardian agreed but told Rick she would have to come back on a different occasion to see him. So Harold and Claire were interviewed, Harold not holding back on how much he disliked me, "She's too immature, doesn't do anything. She's not a good mother at all. Even Ruth is a problem, spoiled rotten. She doesn't care about Jack. Look at Ruth. Mary treats them both the same."

My visit was next. The guardian was very nice, very professional. She looked around the apartment, talked with us all individually, and then the kids together.

At this time Mike and I had become engaged, and found a

home to rent. The family court investigator saw us there. She did the same as the guardian. The kids went to play out in the backyard, and she watched them. The investigator stayed for some time, just taking everything in. We chatted every once in a while, but she seemed to sit and observe more then anything. Months had passed, and still no court date.

The investigator finished her report, eighty-six pages long. It contained the home visits, daycare visits, inquiry to Ruth's elementary school, and some books she used as reference on sibling bonds, and family values. She recommended Jack remain with me.

We were getting anxious to get this over with. The guardian still did not have her report out. This angered Mr.Hooper. He brought it before a judge in presiding court, "Your Honor, we have been waiting for this report. We want to get this to superior court. She needs to be forced to put out her investigation report."

The guardian was unable to be there but had a representative speak for her: "Your Honor, I am here on the guardian's behalf, and the time to finish her report has been delayed, because the father, the plaintiff rather, requested two home visits. She is very busy, and to do the two visits at the plaintiff's home proved difficult. It took some time to get back over to talk with the father. Her report will be out within the next two weeks."

Mr.Hooper argued, "Your Honor, that was too long of a time span for her visitation. I feel it could damage her opinion."

The judge looked tired, "Counsel, you've got two competent investigators. I'm sure the time span won't hurt anything."

"I want a third opinion" Mr. Hooper said, "I feel that's owed to my client."

"No," the judge said. "There has already been so much time spent on this case, let's just get a court date filed."

Mr. hooper was persistent, "Your Honor, I will be out of town for the next two weeks. Give us that time for a third report."

The judge then agreed. "I don't see the point but you have two weeks. What is your suggestion?"

"A psychologist, court-referred would be fine." Rick and his attorney picked a man that was on the court's list of area psychologists. I was ordered to visit him three times.

When I met Dr. Tyman, I was pretty nervous. I thought my attorney should have done more than let this guy slip into the case. Rick was paying the charges for the visits, about twelve hundred dollars. Dr. Tyman saw Rick and me separately. On one of my visits, I took a mental health test and the doctor chatted with Jack. He did this on one of Rick's visits, as well. Through the conversation and some play activities, Doctor Tyman was able to make an assessment of Jack, that he was a smart and wonderful child.

He was also able to do that with Rick and me from just two one-hour appointments that were nothing but questions about the time Rick and I lived together. He brought up only once the subject of my children, and their relationship to one another. He brought up once, how I felt about Rick as a primary parent.

I replied "Rick is a good dad. I believe he really does care for Jack. But Rick isn't able to carry the full responsibilities of being a 'single parent'. He lives with his parents. So Grandma and Grandpa take a lot of the caregiving duties. Rick needs them to care for him also. He's lived there all his life."

The doctor took some notes, "So, Mary, this is bad? Because of Rick's living arrangements, you feel he is incapable of raising Jack? That makes you the better parent, huh?"

I could see where this was going. Rick's paying the bill, so what side is the doctor on? Doctor Tyman never suggested he needed to see the kids together. He never made an effort to contact the other experts involved in my case.

His recommendation was out one week after the visitations were completed. Before I could know his opinion, Doctor Tyman offered to mediate for Rick and me.

"Mary, I suggested it to Rick already, and he's willing. I tell you, this can solve everything and keep it out of court, which by the way, is going to cost thousands in attorney fees."

I called Mr. Chan, "Doctor Tyman says he'll mediate for us and get us to a conclusion so we can stay out of court. What do you think"?

"I don't know. Mr. Chan replied. "Whatever you're comfortable with. The guardian's report is out and she has recommended that Jack stay with you. I already have Tyman's report and know where he stands, but if you want to mediate, I'll have to wait to tell you. If you decide you are going to do it, make sure they understand you are the primary parent."

I couldn't help but think of the money I could save, and knowing the two investigator's reports, how could Rick see otherwise. I agreed to meet with Rick and Dr. Tyman.

At our mediation session Doctor Tyman began, "Mary, you feel you should have Jack primarily, and Rick, you feel you should. Mary why do you feel that way?"

I explained, "Not only do I love Jack, but I want my kids together. I want to raise them both. I feel Rick, you living with your parents, isn't how Jack should be raised.

"Jack's not even four yet. He still needs his mom. If later, when he gets in his teens, and he wants to live with Rick, he has that option."

Tyman looked to Rick, "How about you, Rick. What's your reason?"

Rick began,"Well, I think the son should stay with the father. Jack's known my parent's house the most, Mary, you've moved twice since we split. And Jack's getting to make friends in the neighborhood."

Doctor Tyman questioned me, "Mary, what's wrong with that? Rick seems to have many reasons in Jack's best interest. Why can't you be a little more open-minded, and see a father being the primary parent? Do you think because you're the mother that automatically makes you better? Think of all the pluses Rick provides."

I was amazed; I knew what Doctor Tyman's decision was now, and it was interfering with our 'mediation'. "Doctor Tyman", I said hotly, "I thought you were mediating. You're obviously being biased to Rick. It's you two men against me. Well, I guess we'll have to let a judge decide, because you are not staying down the middle like you're supposed to be."

I got up and Tyman and Rick sat there staring up at me, with no words. I left, feeling like nothing would stop me in court. All this bswould come out in court, and a judge would see that Jack belonged with me and his sister.

When I arrived home I called Mr. Chan, "It didn't go well. Doctor Tyman was trying to convince me why Rick should be the primary."

Mr. Chan agreed, "I didn't think anything would come of it. Tyman recommends the father for reasons that a son should be with the father, he's lived in that home mainly, lots of kids in the neighborhood, and support of the grandparents."

Those were just about identical to Ricks reasonings at mediation. Mr. Chan continued, "Tyman also recommends that Rick seek some counseling to strengthen his parenting skills. He's sending him to a guy that specializes in how to be a better parent."

I asked, "How can he recommend Rick as primary parent only to say he needs better parenting skills? And how come he gets to give that kind of advice when he's only supposed to write a report and recommendation based on our visits?"

Mr. Chan didn't have an answer. I couldn't see the fairness.

So Rick visited with a counselor and read some books. I knew his attorney would be sure to bring this up to the judge. I thought it showed Rick's parenting difficulties, instead of how able he was, so I didn't worry much about it.

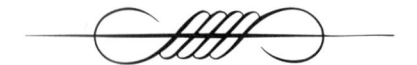

Court day had finally arrived. The courtroom was gloomy. It had a musty smell to it. The bailiff appeared, "All rise for the Honorable Judge Dee."

His Honor came out from an opened room by the jury box. He was elderly with gray hair, and he walked slowly to his seat. I could see that his hearing aid practically covered his ear. Mr. Chan and I sat at a table to the right of the judge; Rick and Mr. Hooper were to the left.

Because Rick was the petitioner, he and his attorney would speak first. Mr. Hooper discussed Rick's family, saying how close they all were to each other. He talked with Rick about how we met, our dating and about the time Rick was told of my pregnancy. "Rick, what did you think?"

Rick said, "Shock. We still saw each other, though. I was overwhelmed that she was going to have a baby."

Mr. Hooper asked, "Do you remember Jack's first year? How did you participate?"

Rick answered, "Yes. We were very close. I took care of him the majority of the time, changing the diapers, feeding him, rocking him to sleep, dressing him, bathing, washing his hair, taking him to the doctor when needed. I basically took care of him."

Mr. Hooper asked, "Why is that? Why did you handle all his needs?"

Rick replied, "I thought Mary seemed overburdened, that

the two kids were too much for her. Mary basically turned Jack over to me when I was home. I started taking him to church with me since he was two weeks old."

Mr. Hooper smiled, "Did Mary ever attend with you?"

Rick answered, "I think there was one Easter and one Christmas that she attended church."

I thought Rick was ridiculous, that he sat up there and said those things. He knows very well that I participated in church many times with him. We had Jack baptized there; you must be a parishioner to participate in baptism.

I will admit, though, church was sometimes difficult for me. It had such a routine, that I felt I didn't learn anything at all. I achieved more from reading out of the Bible or something from Billy Graham. Rick was a robot about church, especially when his parents were around. In fact the first year we were together, I met him at a playfield every Sunday morning to watch him practice, then play a game of flag football. Then his buddies and he went to a bar and grill to have a breakfast of steak and eggs.

I told my attorney of my recollection, hoping to show that Rick wasn't this perfect churchgoer as he and Mr. Hooper were heavily relying on.

Mr. Hooper continued with his questions, "Did Jack ever come down with chicken pox?"

"Yes, he did."

"And when was that?"

"He was about eight months old."

"What happened? What did Mary do?"

"Ruth had come down with it first. Mary asked if I could stay home from school that night. Ruth didn't seem sick to me, so I went to school. And later on, Jack had come down with it pretty bad. He had it all over his face, his chest, his stomach, his bottom and legs. He had them everywhere."

"Okay. So who took care of him?"

"I did. Mary seemed to be a bit squeamish about the sores on him. She said she didn't like them; it didn't matter to me though. I think Jack missed that physical and emotional attention from Mary."

I wanted to scream. I truly was amazed at his testimony. Did he really forget that I was down with chicken pox also? That day he came home from work, I had been sent home because of the dots on my face. I was worried because I had never had the pox and had heard that it can be more serious for adults than children. Yes I wanted him to stay home from school to keep Jack from Ruth and me.

I was "a bit squeamish" about the sores? Give me a break. So I had Rick help put lotion on Jack's sores. That doesn't mean I was freaky. I handled Ruth's sores, and when Rick was around I asked him to help with Jack. I tried to get the feeling of defending myself immediately on the testimony out of my mind. I knew my lawyer would cross examine Rick, and the judge would hear the whole story.

We were in our second day of court, and still, Mr. Hooper continued to have direct with Rick. Other testimony was brought in here and there, according to witnesses' time schedules. The Family Court Investigator had made her appearances as well as Mr. Tyman.

Rick had some neighbor witnesses, a couple of women, and a lady teaching Sunday School that Rick had put Jack in last year. In the end, Rick's testimony had made me out to be a mother who took absolutely no participation in her baby's life. According to Rick, Ruth and I were not important to Jack. Jack never talked about us or seemed to miss us.

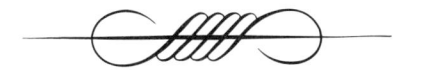

According to Rick, he had done it all. He worked full time, he went to school one night a week, he studied one day every weekend, and he liked to work out at the gym whenever he could. He was a stable church-going man who had lived with his parents all his life, and with all this, he was the main caregiver to our son, the only one who really did anything. I was hopeful that we would show how Rick only played a minor role, and, because of me, Rick began to participate in Jack's caregiving.

I wanted to finish the stories that Rick had partially forgotten and to show what a powerful position the grandparents, Claire and Harold, actually did play, not only in Jack's life, but also Rick's. The whole ordeal was wearing me down. Going into our third day, I hadn't slept much, was vomiting, and had a fever. I wasn't up for it anymore. Driving up to the courthouse left me with a terrible stomach ache. I hoped this would be the last day.

Mr. Chan cross-examined Rick. He was choppy, inconsistent. Mr. Chan wasn't bringing up questions I felt were important to ask Rick. When he was finished, he sat down next to me, "Mr. Chan," I said, "why don't you ask Rick why he's lived at home all his life? What are his plans for the future? I wanted you to ask things that would show how much Claire and Harold really do most of the caring for my son at that house."

He whispered into my ear, "Mary, don't worry, those things are insignificant to the judge. It wouldn't matter much."

I was worried; Mr. Chan didn't bring up the chicken pox and Rick's schedule. I felt the load on my shoulders. My testimony would be very important. I would have to get all my thoughts out that Mr. Chan couldn't. I hoped I would remember.

Mr. Chan interviewed my mother, the daycare provider, even Michael, who by this time was my husband. They helped shed some light on my parenting, and how much the kids meant to me. Then it was my turn. I was nervous, with all the people in the courtroom staring at me. I hoped I would be able to speak smoothly, clearly.

Mr. Chan began, "Mary, describe parenting functions between Rick and yourself."

So I began, I told of Rick's work schedule and that he roomed in the basement, of my illness that prompted him to move upstairs. I talked about his job move, and me starting back to work.

Mr. Chan posed a question, "Now, you have heard the allegation or assertion you refused to do parenting functions?"

"Yes."

"And the father had to change diapers, do the cooking and do the baths and et cetera, et cetera, for Jack."

"Right."

"And that you refused to do these things. What's your response?"

I stumbled over my words."Well, I respond that that is absolutely not true. I was tending to the kids by myself upstairs.

"It wasn't until I got ill that I got more help. It took me a few months to get on my feet. And, I just, I did with the kids just as I normally would but just maybe with some help from Rick."

I couldn't get what I wanted to say to come out the same I was thinking it. My fingers were cold. My mouth was dry. I was sweating, I felt like I was going to vomit. Should I ask to be excused?

Mr. Chan continued wanting me to describe my daily routine when I had the kids. I was feeling confused. I described the kids' day as best I could. I answered questions about me and Rick's relationship, Rick's work schedule, the fire at the house.

We discussed Jack's schedule after our split, and why it was that way, I answered it this way, "Well, at that time I was, when I started working full-time, I was full-blown into six days a week and I tried for Jack's sake, I tried thinking of a schedule where he could be with his father and myself that he was used to."

"Is this the schedule you worked out?" Mr.Chan asked.

"Yeah, it was nothing, uh, written or anything, but at that time with me trying to get back on my feet as being a single person again and getting out on my own, this is how I dealt with it, thinking this was the best for Jack at the time."

I made it through my direct examination from Mr. Chan. He finished up with me discussing my use of the daycare, the relationship between my children, our home, our family activities. I brought in pictures of the kids at different ages together, Mr.Chan used those as exhibits for the judge.

"Now, briefly can you describe your relationship between Jack and yourself." Mr. Chan asked.

"Well, I have, I feel like I have a really good relationship with both my children and I've carried that on from Ruth to Jack. Jack and I get along really well. He's a really good little boy. The relationship between him and me, has to kind of almost , even though, well, I don't know how to explain it. When he comes back(from his dad's) he's a little bit different. He sometimes forgets, calls me grandma and it takes a little bit, a while, to almost remember where he is. But once we get back into the family routine, if he's got a problem, he comes to me."

I went on, completely nervous."We try to talk things out if he's angry at something. If there's any kind of argument between him and his sister, they are split apart and we try to figure out what's going on. I just feel like, the relationship between all of us is just really strong."

Mr. Hooper was ready to cross-examine me. He started off with questioning me about my reasons for having Jack at daycare. Why was I opposed to the grandparents watching him? He talked about the importance of the kids who lived near the grandparents home, saying they were beneficial to Jack. We talked about my financial statements, and my suggested parenting plan. He asked if I had told Rick about my husband and me trying to buy a home.

"You didn't tell Rick that you and Mike were marrying, did you?"

"No, I don't think I did."

"And yet you say that you believe that joint-decision making should be the way to go in this case?"

"My getting married to a man is not part of my decision-making with Rick."

"Wouldn't you agree that joint-decision-making means full disclosure to the other parent, keeping them informed of important events like marriage and moving?"

"Rick always knew where we were moving and he also knew that I had a very strong relationship with my husband. I just assumed he would probably assume it was going to turn into marriage, but I didn't feel I had to confide in him."

"And you blame communication problems on my client?"

"I don't believe I blamed anything like that."

That was that. I was off the stand, but didn't feel very good about it all. It had been long, and I didn't have a sense of things being resolved. Mr. Chan felt pretty good about things, but I remained nervous.

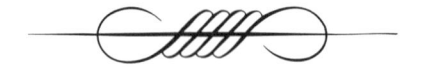

———⚜———

Mr. Hooper decided to call Rick's dad, Harold, to the stand. I was surprised. Mr. Hooper just wanted to know about the daycare situation.

"Now, you're around in the morning when Jack gets up, according to your testimony. Does he jump out of bed, excited to get ready for daycare?"

"Usually he's not anxious to go to daycare, no."

"Why not? Why do you think that is so?"

"I think he just feels comfortable and secure at home. He's always lived there and he enjoys being there."

Mr. Hooper was finished. Mr. Chan got up and asked, "You say Jack gets up in the morning around seven a.m.?"

"Yeah, he usually sleeps until seven, sometimes later."

"You're there at that time?"

"Yes."

"Okay. Is Rick there also?"

"No, Rick's gone to work by that time."

"Okay. And so you and your wife fix breakfast and change him and get Jack ready to go in the morning?"

"Yes."

Mr. Chan didn't go any further. Both attorneys expressed each was finished, there was no further questioning.

The judge had some questions and words of his own. He asked about a financial obligation I had on my report and if it was from my relationship with Rick. He wanted to know if my husband had any support due from another relationship. Then he spoke of the case.

"I'll be making a decision probably in writing, and my decision is from time to time reviewed by a higher authority. I would like to share with any other reviewing authority somewhat of the flavor of the testimony."

"Counsel," he continued, go to your offices, get your closing arguments written and sent out to me within seven days. Then I'll respond with a written decision and my reasons."

He went on, "I want you to both know, as long as the parties are here, that this is a very difficult decision. You both are decent people, making this a hard decision to make."

There was a long silence before he continued, "On occasion, in a case like this, what I have ended up doing, is I write up two decisions, one favoring either side, and after I get the decision written, justifying that conclusion, weighing the balance at that point, well, I might have to do that in this case. Thank you."

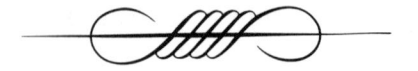

Two weeks later, I finally heard from my attorney while I was at work.

"Mary, I got the judge's decision."

My heart skipped a beat, "Really? Bad news, huh?" I said jokingly.

"Yes, I'm afraid so" he replied.

My heart sank. I began to cry. "Read me what he sent you." So he did.

Gentlemen;

I have considered all the testimony, the exhibits admitted, and now have had the benefit of counsels' closing arguments. For many reasons, the most important of which I will try to explain, I have concluded that the child will be best served with his father as primary custodian. I feel both parents would provide a sufficient home, and that both are caring. I feel the father showed total devotion and commitment to his son; this impressed me, they have a bond which should not be broken. The experts when speaking of the children, missed their mark of the sibling bond. They are not full-siblings; they are half, and this does make a difference. Jack will always have two homes, where Ruth will have one. This is regardless of who is primary custodial parent.

In any event, the children are going to have much of the time away from each other. Full siblings, normally, will accompany each other during visitation, making it easier to divide their time between two homes. In this case, only Jack suffers/benefits from dividing his time between two parents. The children's bond is broken, and there is no way to keep them together.

I also feel that the father is going to be more giving to the mother when it comes to visitation. The father will be pliable with the visitation needs of a working mother and her growing family, also of an active boy. If I am wrong in this regard, the father turns out unreasonable, doesn't follow the legal form, that would be just cause to re-look at the custody issue. I do not want to endanger the child's mental health, over visitation quarreling or post co-habitation.

With respect to visitation, I would suggest alternate weekends, a day visit mid-week, and reasonable phone contact. Divide major holidays and summer break. Support shall be pursuant to the guidelines adopted in this county. Any unanswered details can be discussed, if not now, upon presentation of findings."

Four years have gone by now as I write this, since a judge made his decision to give primary custody of my son, Jack, to my former boyfriend. I have struggled with many things, myself as a mother as well as a person. I have gone through many emotions: shock, sadness, anger, and regret that I wasn't as strong of a person as I probably needed to be. Of course, if we could all see our lives in hindsight before it actually happens, we would all be prepared for situations that arise in our lives, able to make changes. That is why I am writing these things.

'Part 1: The Story', is very difficult, very personal, and was hard to lay down on paper. 'Part 2: Reference', is for anyone in a similar situation. Hopefully you can gain insight, an understanding that if a legal matter comes before you, you must be strong and take as much of the matter into your own hands as you can.

Understand that communication, or at least the trying of it, can be a key to resolving things, leaving you with the knowledge and understanding of your own circumstance.

Unfortunately, many cases will go before a court that could have been resolved simply by speaking to one another. Even when talking it out is rough, there are many things that can be tried before relying on an attorney, and then a judge, for an outcome.

With so many attorneys and bitter people, it is easy to see how we have lost control of thoughts and feelings, and feel fighting is the only way to get things done.

Above all, don't lose sight of the children involved. Take a deep breath and be honest with yourself. What do you really want? What do you want for the kids, no matter how you feel about the other parent. Educate yourself in the area you are having a problem with. Look at things that are passing you by, learn from them, listen to your instincts on what path to take. Have faith.

Part Two
Reference
*Help Yourself
Knowledge Equals Power*

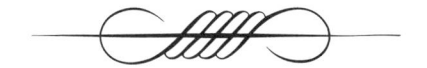

If I had only stepped back and took a breath of reality after finding myself getting into a custody battle, I would have been better off. When we are in the midst of divorce or separation, we automatically feel we are on the defense. The only way to defend ourselves, we reason, is by having an attorney.

An attorney was the only way to handle my situation, I felt. I didn't think I had any other choice.

Lawyers can be a big help with property disbursement, assets, and legal loopholes. And when the disputing parties are unable to communicate due to anger, sadness or just plain revenge, a lawyer might do well for you.

But be aware of the pitfalls, too. When retaining an attorney, I found that the words of confidence that poured from my attorney's lips made me feel assured that the issues of custody would be solved easily. So I set those issues aside and dealt with the other things of my life.

When you split from the other party, or have a child and are on your own, other things keep you busy; work, other family members, friends, debts, yourself. You figure, this lawyer knows what they're talking about. And Lord knows, I'm paying them enough! You begin to rely on, or even hide behind them, because you feel they can get you through this.

Attorneys do charge a great amount, anywhere from $75.00 to $185.00 per hour. Why so much? Is it because of all that schooling, studying and tests? I don't know. Attorneys are a dime a dozen these days, and you'd think with so many, there would be a price reduction from all the competition. If you feel you must have an attorney, check around.

Get references from friends, and relatives. Look in the yellow pages or use a lawyer referral office that has a 1-800 number. Talk with an attorney who specializes in the area you need. For example, most attorneys dabble in a little bit of everything, but if you are seeking help in the area of family law, make sure that the lawyer you talk with is most experienced in that field.

Don't rely on an attorney who has done some family law issues, whose primary work is with personal injury cases.

When speaking with an attorney for a consultation, many will either have no fee or charge half of their hourly rate. Some may just have a minimal cost for the first visit. If you have the time and some money to spare, my opinion would be to visit as many different attorneys you can. Find out how long they have been in law and how many cases they have had that would be similar to your situation.

Ask them anything you can think of that you have concerns about, or that you are curious about. Find a lawyer you are comfortable with.

Don't let their egos or smooth talk win you over. Granted, those characteristics can be useful when they talk in the courtroom, but it also can lead to such overconfidence that the lawyer might put your case on the back burner and not prepare properly for the trial.

And remember, you are not the only client the lawyer will have. If you find an attorney you like, ask what kind of workload they have. Will they have time for you? Can you call with problems or questions and have their full attention?

Compare an attorney this way. When you have a doctor visit, then get the bill, you see it was an expensive trip. Was the doctor helpful? If you have to see the doctor again and several times more, you want your money's worth, right? You certainly wouldn't keep seeing the doctor and paying his/her fees if you didn't have the results you wanted or expected. That's the same with a lawyer. You want action. You want assurance that something is being done and properly handled. Remember, it's your money. You don't get a tax break or any reimbursement on it; it's just out of your pocket into the attorney's.

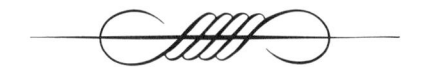

With divorce, sometimes custody of the kids is not such an issue. It's been said that, occasionally, the threat of a custody fight from the father is a ploy to try and get a better divorce deal, "I'll drop the custody issue if you give the car to me." Why does a father desire custody of the children?

I've been told anywhere from, "Just because you're a woman doesn't mean you should get the kids" or "I can do just as well of a job raising the kids as the mother. Besides I don't want to see my kids just every other weekend and holidays."

Another reason for a father to fight is they feel rejected.

The father 'winning' custody will make him powerful, that the failed relationship with the mother, no matter what reason, makes him feel like the better person. I had a father tell me once that having custody of his children was showing the mother that she didn't hold all the cards.

Well, whatever the argument, I feel the children should remain primarily with the mother when a split of the parents occurs. If you have an unfit mother, abusive, using drugs, overusing alcohol, or the children are at such an age that they can voice where they prefer to live, then you have a different case.

I believe a father has an important role in his child's life, regardless if it's a boy or girl. But no man will ever know or experience the pregnancy, labor and birth of that baby and when you have a mother who has gone through all of that patiently and who has shared her body so that another human being can be brought into this world, we must try and understand the bond that develops.

If women are losing custody because they use a daycare center while they work, or they work and go to school, even if it's because they have remarried and have other children making half siblings for the child at issue, then I feel we are being told by some of the judges who make these decisions that we women must revert back to the 1800s and stay at home, cooking and cleaning. If I cannot balance it all, children and life outside the home, am I unworthy?

I wonder, if a pregnant woman was told that after her child was born, somewhere down the line she would become an every-other-weekend mother due to a custody dispute, what would she do? Are women going to be scared to have children for that reason? Are women going to have agreements drawn up and have the fathers sign it saying that if their relationship doesn't work out, the father cannot retain full custody?

And we want fathers as well as mothers involved in their children's lives. But when the father does some caregiving, enough to convince a judge that the father is in the best interest of the child, will mothers feel they need to worry about putting restrictions on how much the father is involved?

For years Judges let custody cases side quickly in the mother's defense. However, in the 1970s, men started arguing that it was discrimination, that their Fourteenth Amendment rights were being violated. The courts had the problems of fathers putting the pressure on, so more and more fathers now retain custody. Don't think it can't happen to you.

Think of your life right now, whether you are living with your child's father or not. Think about your daily schedule. How do you balance it all? Work, bills, the kids, yourself, friends. Feel like it's hectic? But you feel you're doing all right? You're a good person, a good mom, you try really hard. Right?

That's not going to always make it, though, if you are headed to the courthouse for a custody fight. If the father wants the custody of the kids, he and his attorney will not hold back. They will bring up anything insignificant against you and will blow it out of proportion if they have to.

Child custody cases go as far back as the late seventeenth century. Divorce itself was a difficult issue. Women who requested it, usually were denied. When spousal abuse and extreme adultery could be shown on the wife's behalf, divorce became an easier subject to deal with and grant.

Children were looked upon as possessions, and in common law, the father received all possessions after a separation of husband and wife. You can imagine an infant being breast-fed by its mother, and then taken away from her due to the separation. What a harsh rule.

Women, going through a divorce with young children involved, began to argue at the loss of their minor children. Attorneys pleaded with judges to understand the tender years of a child and how they would benefit from remaining with their mother. Two statements came from those arguments: the tender years doctrine and the maternal preference. Judges began to automatically award primary custodial rights to the mother unless it was proven that she was unfit, having a mental illness or was abusive to the children.

Through the years those two statements have been mandated by most states, that no courts may take them into consideration when deciding a custody case.

Have you ever thought about the judge's position? How does

a judge become a judge? If you are a voter, think about the ballot. Do you vote for a candidate just because their name sounds nice?

What do we know about the people who run for a seat on the bench? Many of the judicial candidates are recommended by the bar association, lawyers giving their ratings on who we should consider to vote for.

A person who has never set foot in front of a judge, doesn't think much about it. I know I didn't. But to become a judge, there is no big campaign challenge, no need for a list of achievements in dealing and understanding the law. In fact a judge can remain on the bench until the day he or she dies.

What is the basic definition of 'child custody'? It's the parent who has the legal responsibilities to care for that child on a day-to-day basis. That parent also has the right to make any major decisions regarding the child. If joint custody is agreed upon, then both parents have the right to major decision-making and the child usually spends equal time with both parents.

If your case goes before a judge, the judge is to decide what is in the "best interest of the child." This statement does not have any clear definition to it. It is up to a judge what it means. A judge may feel a father is in the "best interest" of a child if the child is a boy.

Now, that shouldn't be the deciding factor, should it? But it can be, and the judge would likely phrase it in such a way so it doesn't look biased. Judges have a wide range in decision making when it comes to deciding family issues. That's why I say to you mothers, it can happen to you. You can lose primary care of your children.

If the father and mother are to be considered good parents,

with no drug use, neglect or abuse, the judge has a free rein, so to speak, on where the children will primarily reside. This is decided by which party can best prove who has been most responsible in caring for the child since birth. It's like a play; which side's role will impress the judge the most?

I feel when the father and his attorney show different situations where the father has had a hand in caring for the child, a diaper change, bath time, feeding time, and maybe even cooking dinner, this can make a judge feel better about granting custody to the father. Does it make a man greater, in the best interest of the child, when he helps out with the tasks at hand?

I wonder if a judge, when presented with such evidence, makes his or her decision based on those times, because they feel it's so extraordinary that a father participates in the child care for whatever reason. Remember, the judge has the right to consider all if any evidence and information in your case. For all you know, a judge may be using their own private experiences to help decide your case. Worded properly, an appeal on the decision is unlikely.

If you become the non-custodial parent, here are some things you should expect. You will be responsible for child support. The amount will be determined by a scale. It looks like a tax table to me.

The guidelines will take into consideration both parties' income, as well as other children involved. It is your state's guidelines, structured to approximate what both parents would be contributing to the child support if separation of the parents had not occurred.

Non-custodial payment is based on the child's age; it can be raised as the child gets older. Child support is a sticky subject to me. A non-custodial parent doesn't have any say on where the support goes.

The primary parent can spend it how they choose. It might mean a new car, new clothes, nights out, and the child may be missing out on that new winter coat. If both parents are financially responsible, how come only one gets the say of how it's spent?

Non-custodial parents normally don't get tax deduction for child-support payments; it's under the table so to speak.

Support guidelines need more attention to them. Society has become used to hearing about the deadbeat parents that don't pay. I admit, there are many situations where children are suffering because of the lack of financial backing.

We need to focus on what it really costs to support a child, and how those funds are being spent. We need to remember the paying parent's needs also. I overheard a father complaining of his situation. He admitted he has two children, and he should financially help out. He hadn't been working, not taking any responsibilities for his kids. Now he has a job. The state was garnishing his wages. So much that he couldn't pay for the tabs on his car. No tabs, no driving. No driving, no work. The bus was suggested. Not a stop he could easily walk to. A friend, family member? No one close. See how it can unravel? This type of situation, unfortunately, makes some people give up all together.

There are non-custodial parents paying as little as $25.00 a month to thousands a month. There needs to be a balance, so bitter feelings of the all mighty dollar doesn't affect the child/parent relationship.

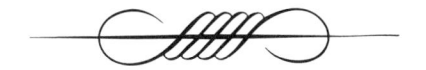

Your visitation schedule would likely be every other weekend, Friday to Sunday. A weeknight, four hours. Half of the child's school breaks, winter, spring and summer, and alternation of major holidays. The judge will probably give their opinion on what they feel would be best for the child, which is usually the standard schedule. All this will be put into a parenting plan. It becomes a bible for your parenting rights.

Other things can be added to the plan: Tax dependent claims, visitation on the child's birthday as well as the parent's birthday, telephone contact, religious and educational decisions, and daycare costs.

This type of parenting plan, although it's the standard, isn't right for everyone. I think that the parenting plan should change to reflect the child's age and relationship he or she has with their parent. And you can do that.

Every weekend might work. Time after school Monday through Friday could be another possibility for some parents. If it is not confusing or frustrating the child, different options should be explored.

For myself, it has been very difficult only to be able to see my son every other weekend. Going to any sporting or schooling events he is in has been helpful.

As I have done with my daughter, I have also done with my son, volunteering to help in his classroom during school time. I have seen his excitement and sometimes he has acted like he doesn't care that I'm there, until it's time for me to leave. I feel he is appreciative of me, to see me other than of the scheduled times. It helps get me through the week until he is back home on my weekend.

Don't think the child or children are always fine with the arrangements of seeing one parent every other weekend. I think it must be very difficult for a child to have both parents in their life, then because mom and dad's relationship doesn't work out, the child all of a sudden doesn't have one of their parents around as often. So, if you are a non-custodial parent, take time for your child other than what's in the parenting plan, unless there are good enough reasons why you shouldn't.

Are you unmarried and pregnant? Of course it's easier if you are in a situation where there is no question of who the father is, but whether you have that problem or not, establishing paternity at the child's birth is very important.

Regardless if the father wants to partake in the child's life or not, signing a paternity affidavit will legalize the father and will help enforce his support.

With the affidavit being signed by both parents, the child will have many benefits: insurance, inheritance, social security, and death or disability benefits.

At the time of the baby's birth, the hospital staff should be able to provide an affidavit to the unmarried parents. The hospital can help complete and notarize the forms for up to ten days after the child's birth.

By signing the affidavit, the form can be presented to a support enforcement office if the parents aren't together. This presumption of paternity created by the father signing the affidavit allows a child support process to begin.

Women, before agreeing to signing an affidavit, make certain the baby's father is the actual father. Sometimes the system fails, and child support will be garnished from a man's wages because a woman has turned him in as the father to Support Enforcement. Start a petition for blood work on the assumed father and the child in question.

Mothers, I also suggest you contact your local prosecutor's office. Often they can help a mother who has a paternity affidavit. They can set up child support and also draft up a parenting plan. They will serve the father with the papers.

If the father agrees but wants some different issues addressed in the parenting plan, they will try and accommodate for both parties and what would best suit the child. This can be a time and money saver for both parents.

But what if the parents cannot agree on the issue of custody and/or visitation? It can be a difficult road if the father hires an attorney and serves the mother with papers petitioning that he be the custodial parent and requests a court hearing in the matter.

Don't panic. You can seek out an attorney and speak with them as I've stated before. But understand, when you make that commitment, it will be long and difficult. In many cases, a judge won't hear your case for up to a year. You must wait your turn on the court's long list.

I understand that may be the only road to take. But before you do, think about another option: mediation.

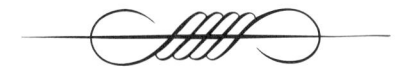

With mediation, both parties meet with an unbiased third party, the mediator, attending to assist in communication, and negotiations. A mediator can be a person from the mental health industry, a psychologist, an attorney, or someone who practices mediation as a profession.

You can find them in the yellow pages. There is also an organization, The Dispute Resolution Center(DRC), who provides trained people as mediators. A mediator will charge by the hour, ranging from $25.00 to $85.00. The DRC charges a fee based on the parties' income. They provide services in many states.

First, mediation lets both parties speak what is on their minds, getting issues out in the open. For instance, with a custody issue, the parties will be heading for court to await a judge's decision on where the child will primarily reside. Lawyers are involved, and there is a lot of tension between both sides. With the tension and all the concerns you may have for your child, you can express it all in mediation.

Try to communicate with the other party. A good mediator will help assist in that goal. They will help identify the issues, generate options, and bring about a settlement.

It is not the mediator's part to decide what or who is right or wrong, but to make it possible for the parties to create their own written and binding agreements.

I have given you some suggestions on where you might find a mediator. It may be a little difficult, because you want to make sure that if the parties are willing to meet for a mediation session, you are both comfortable with the choice.

One might feel on the defense if the other party found an attorney they liked, for instance, and asked them for mediation help without consulting the other party. I prefer the DRC.

Here in Washington, they provide two mediators, one male and one female. The DRC has earned a national reputation as a leader in dispute resolutions. The trainees learn essential conflict resolution skills through lectures, demonstrations, and exercises. Trainees have included individuals nationwide and public, private corporations and Federal/State and local government agencies.

You can see mediation can be used in many different situations but all going for the same goal, communication with results.

Think about mediation if you are having a child custody conflict. You may also be able to use mediation for a divorce. You and the other parent may not get along very well. Unfortunately, you may have resentment towards that person.

But you have to remember, you are going to have to deal with this person on many occasions, for the sake of the child you have both created. Instead of leaving the final decision to a judge, you can help make that decision with the other parent.

Mediation is on a voluntary basis. If both parties can go in with an open mind and discuss things at a mature level, the results can be very gratifying, saving hundreds even thousands of dollars in court costs.

Mediation is confidential. The mediators can give legal information, but not legal advice. Mediation may be inappropriate if the case presents constitutional or precedent-setting issues which should be heard through the courts.

It may not be advisable if a party is unable to negotiate due to substance abuse, psychological impairment, physical or emotional abuse by the other party. These problems can be addressed with an attorney present.

Attorneys may attend a mediation session with the client, and issues may be brought out during the mediation and discussed. Mediators can help the parties create solutions, but it is the parties who share in the outcome.

The resolution process can be time consuming. If the parties refuse each other's desires, be prepared for long sessions. When an agreement is formed, your mediator should make sure there are no other issues that are concerning each party. Everything should be out on the table and understood. The agreement will be drafted by the mediator. The issues and the agreed conclusion will be written down.

The mediators will sign the statement, and each party should thoroughly read the papers before signing. The language should be understandable and reflect the parties' wishes. Everyone receives a copy. A copy will be retained at the mediator's office if other issues arise or if problems occur with the current agreement. Remember, you can always go back to mediation.

I wish that when attorneys visited with their clients and saw the potential for amicable communication between the parties, they would suggest mediation. But that's not what they are in the business for, is it? So before you retain an attorney, before things get messy and expensive, think about mediation. It can't hurt to try, and if you end up going to court over the issues, a judge will be respectful of your efforts.

Counseling is another resource. It can help you through the situation, and help the child / children involved. Counseling can help you help your child. It is another option that should be explored, taking into consideration the costs and finding one that you and your family are comfortable with. A counselors opinion and suggestions are also good points that can be brought up in coming to an agreement of the issues at hand.

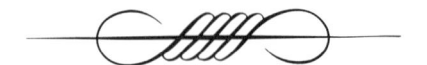

What if down the line you start having problems with your divorce papers, or your parenting plan? You try mediation, because you either can't afford or don't want to deal with a lawyer. But mediation didn't work. Now what? Well, before you get that attorney involved, think of another option.

There was a change in my parenting plan; when my son started full-time schooling, my weekend visitation changed from Friday till Monday morning, to Friday till Sunday night. I was open to this, because I knew I would have difficulties getting two kids to two different schools on time. But with that change, I wanted some time added elsewhere.

I suggested to the father instead of having every other Wednesday, that I have my son every Wednesday. I would pick him up from school and return him by seven p.m.

The father refused. He said it wouldn't do my son well. I argued I had every other Wednesday as it was. What was the difference, except that we would have more time together? He would not budge.

I called for mediation. An appointment was set and we met and discussed the matter, among a couple other issues, for five hours. The father refused to agree on the Wednesday issue, and laid out my son's school schedule and noted half and non school days.

He said he was open to let me have some of those days as my extra time. I argued it wouldn't be a predictable schedule for my son, all these "here" and "there" times.

But as time went on, I agreed to try the father's suggestion. In the agreement, we had also noted that if things weren't working out we agree to come back to mediation.

For months I tried to work with my son's schedule. There were half days that I couldn't make, and the days I wanted weren't good for the father. I had seen my son maybe six hours extra since our mediation. It was March now, and I again requested mediation. The father declined. He knew I couldn't afford an attorney, and I was at his mercy. He had the parenting plan, he was primary parent, so what could I do?

I went to my local courthouse, where the judge who had made my custody decision resided. I hated to walk in there. I was very uncomfortable.

I went to the law library to see if I could read up on something that could help me. A new program had started in the courthouse in a room just across from the library. It was called the family law facilitator's office. It had a line all the way out the door, down half the hallway. I picked up a pamphlet to read about what it offered.

It turns out that many people try to handle things on their own. They try to represent themselves in court. Judges had become frustrated with incorrect paperwork, and it was creating a jumbled-up process.

The courthouse clerks found themselves being asked by people, to guide them through the steps. More times then not, the clerks were not available for the process. Many cases that were going before a judge were being dismissed because of the paperwork problem. That is why the courthouse facilitators office was formed.

So many people wanting changes to help themselves and their children were taking the plunge to speak before a judge, going in almost blindly. The facilitator's office was formed for those reasons. Facilitators aren't available in all states and counties. But I foresee that they will be, due to the overwhelming need. People want to help themselves, in simple situations.

People are tired of paying high attorney fees for things that they can understand and relay quite well to a judge. In Washington State for instance, fourteen counties provide facilitation help through their courthouse.

Many offices are only a one-person staff who see people on a first-come, first-served basis. You must get in line on a particular day, or call at a certain time and hope to be able to get an appointment. After all the appointments are filled up for the following week, you will need to try the same process over again. That is how big the need is. You should contact your local office for their setup.

A facilitator listens to your concerns that you want to bring before the judge. It might be a modification in your parenting plan or a modification in your child support or a restraining order, a paternity action, even a divorce decree.

If you have an issue or issues that are not legally complicated, a facilitator can guide you through the process. If they feel you had better seek an attorney, they will tell you so.

The facilitator is there to assist you with information you need to properly fill out the forms that are required if you want to file your case. You do pay something. The cost for the forms and any filing fee that has been established by statutes of the state. These are paid to the clerks office.

You basically are doing all the typing that an attorney's clerk would do, saving yourself the high fee for that. You write out a declaration, explaining to the judge why you are asking for the change, why you are there.

I received my packet for a modification of the parenting plan. I filled out all the areas the facilitator directed me to do. My declaration was clear, saying the change of my every other weekend warranted another change. Time: I wanted to have more elsewhere.

I provided the mediation agreement. I showed that the father was not following through and had refused another mediation attempt to resolve it.

While I was at it, I asked for another change: an addition to the parenting plan that requested that if my son had an emergency, or for whatever reason was hospitalized, the parent my son was with would be required to notify the other parent. I note to you I asked the father for his agreement, but he would not sign it on his own, stating it was "just a given" if something was to happen he'd call me.

But because of the past, my son having two visits to the emergency room without my notification, I wasn't going to chance it. If you are going to represent yourself in court, you want to be thorough, and write clearly as if you were speaking to the judge.

Provide anything that will help in your case. Receipts, letters, billings, medical records, signed agreements, parenting plan, all of it will help the judge put the pieces together and he or she will be able to get a clear picture of what's going on.

After completing my forms, I had another appointment with the facilitator to look over my work.

When everything is up to the court's standard, you are given a court date and time. You are responsible to have copies of all the forms, one set served to the other party, one set filed with the courts, and a set for yourself.

You are responsible to confirm your court date. If you do not follow the instructions to do so, the judge will not see you.

After the other parent is served with the court documents, they may reply with their own declaration. The other party must show up for court regardless if they made a declaration or not. My ex-boyfriend did submit papers.

The father would use his attorney, Mr. Hooper, to represent him at court time. As I read through the declaration, it made me nauseated. It reminded me of the days I spent in court with these two men chopping me down when they could. Their declaration touched briefly on my issues. For whatever reasons, they had decided to add a variety of other things. They went more for the cutthroat attempt.

Calling me "relentless" ever since I lost custody, the declaration stated I have been difficult at every step. He made note of how much time I spent with my son at his school which was not in the parenting plan.

He stated that I refused to help pay for my son's private school education, that I have constant demands with offers of compromise.

He said that he, the father, had tried to work with me to increase the visitation time. I steadfastly refused to allow our son to participate in his activities on my visitation time.

He noted we missed my sons last T-ball game. Of course they didn't state we were out of town and although I tried to juggle it, finding it did not bother my then six-year-old son not to attend the game, we went ahead with our plans.

My son would be making his first communion soon, and the father stated that I have refused to cooperate and not bring my son to the church they attend on my Sundays. It states, "She has always been this way." When the medical issue came about, they stated it was "wholly unreasonable for the mother to take the position that I have to immediately notify her."

The father stated that the Dispute Resolution attempt was in good faith by him but not me. My request for having my son every Wednesday is, "potentially detrimental to his best interests. The mother seems to be incapable of understanding that just because she wants extra time that such additional time would be disruptive of our son's routine." They asked that the court dismiss my petition.

I will admit, when you are planning to represent yourself and the other party is using an attorney, it is very intimidating.

When court time arrived, my husband went with me. It was like traffic court, a whole bunch of cases all in one room. I would hear everyone's issues, and they would hear mine. I waited not seeing the other parent or his attorney. After twenty minutes, the attorney arrived alone.

I listened to the other cases before me. The judge was attentive as both sides spoke; he didn't ask too many questions if any at all. He had his decisions right at the tip of his tongue, one woman argued when she heard her outcome, but the judge was firm and told her it was over, that was that.

I decided he must really take time and read through all of the cases before court time, and he was prepared with what he thought of all of them.

When my case was called, I got to speak first. I felt my declaration said it all, and I prayed that the judge took time to read through everything. He talked as having a good grasp on the subject at hand and didn't let too much bull enter the dispute.

As I spoke, Mr. Hooper folded his arms and looked right at

me, for intimidation, I suppose. I plugged along, reiterating bits of my declaration.

Mr. Hooper spoke, immediately apologizing for taking up the judge's time on such insignificant issues, and proposed it be dismissed.

At that moment, I pictured the judge agreeing with Hooper. But the facilitators wouldn't send me this far if I didn't have a chance. The judge defended me, saying it seemed to him I had just cause for wanting additional time. Mr. Hooper seemed shocked and dove into other issues of their declaration that had nothing to do with what was at hand.

He talked about times on my weekends I didn't always attend things the father had set up for my son. The judge lashed out, "The father cannot force the mother to do anything he wants on her weekend. It's her time." Mr. Hooper brought up the communion situation. Again the judge couldn't believe what the attorney was saying.

The judge brought up the mediation factor, and Mr. Hooper didn't have a copy of it. After getting one and looking it over, Mr. Hooper asked that the parties try mediation again, so we didn't have to take up any more of the court's time. The judge read through the mediation agreement and I stated that the father had refused another visit.

The judge told Mr. Hooper, "Your client doesn't seem to be able to attend mediation in good faith. It seems to me the father is frustrating the program. All this mother wants is some time with her son to make up for the change in her every other weekend. What is the father's problem with that?"

Mr. Hooper argued, "It's detrimental, Your Honor. He is already used to a schedule." I piped in that I felt it was worse for my son not to have a specific day and time, that it would be confusing for him.

The judge agreed with me, and even felt I should have my son till eight p.m instead of seven. He also granted into the parenting plan that, if an emergency occurs, the parents are to be notified as soon as possible.

I had been prepared. I had all my paperwork. I didn't become angry and shout. I didn't become melodramatic. I stuck to the issues, and was honest.

I was very thankful for the outcome. They were minor issues, I suppose, but they were not unreasonable.

And the other parent felt more like it was a "get you" type of argument than what it really was: my love and concern for my son.

Was the father really that blind to understand how much I enjoy time with my son, with my kids, for that matter? This all happened just a while ago as I write this, three and a half years since I lost custody.

I take it as a clue of how the rest of my life with my son will be, until he is of age. The other parent will always look and describe me as 'relentless', 'refusing', and 'demanding.'

If you have issues you would like to get before the judge, and you feel you can represent yourself for whatever reasons, check your local courthouse and see if there is a facilitator's office available. If not, check if there are any self-help programs that deal with 'representing your case yourself.'

Talk with someone in the clerk's office, find out if anyone is available to talk about the court process with you. If so, do they provide the proper forms that are to the court's standards

And be sure to read. The courthouse law library can be very helpful, it's free to use and the information can provide you with a better understanding of the law in your particular state.

Remember, whatever family dispute you are involved in-divorce or child custody, you have a say in what happens. If you can keep the communication lines open with the other party, you will likely solve things more quickly, and at little or no cost. If children are involved, this is a much healthier atmosphere for them to live in. Keeping attorneys and the court system out of the picture as much as possible leaves your situation more in your hands, not in the hands of strangers.

Good luck in your situation, keep an open mind, and God bless.

*National Dispute Resolution Organizations:

Academy of Family Mediators
P.O Box 246, Claremont CA 91711

American Arbitration Association
140 S. 51st St., New York NY 10020

American Bar Association - Special Committee on Alternative Means of Dispute Resolution
1800 M St. NW Washington DC 20036

DRC of Snohomish County, Washington State
P.O Box 839, Everett WA. 98206

DRC of Spokane
West 315 Mission #21, Spokane WA. 99201

Neutral Ground
P.O Box 1222, Walla, Walla WA. 99362

Family Mediation Association
5530 Wisconsin Ave. Suite 1250, Chevy Chase MD 20815

Federal Mediation and Conciliation Service
2100 K St. NW, Washington DC 20427

National Association for Community Justice
149- 9th St., San Francisco CA 94103

National Association for Mediation in Education
c/o Mediation Program
425 Amity St., Amherst MA 01002

National Institute of Dispute Resolution
1901 L St., NW Suite 600, Washington DC. 20036

Society of Professionals in Dispute Resolution
1730 Rhode Island Ave., NW Suite 909, Washington DC 20036

Appendix
Recommended Reading

Mediate, Don't Litigate. By Peter Lovenheim

Fair Share Divorce for Women. By Kathleen Miller

Child Custody- Building Agreements That Work. By Mimi E. Lyster

Divorce and Child Custody (Second Edition). By Deanna Peter and Richard L. Strohm

Don't Settle For Less- Women's Guide To Getting A Fair Divorce and Custody Settlement. By Beverly Pekala

The Rights Of Women (Third Edition) By Susan Deller Ross, Isabelle Katz-Pinzler, Deborah A. Ellis and Kary L. Moss

A Guide To Divorce Mediation. By Gary J. Friedman J.D

Resources/Bibliography

Reference Book: *The Guide To American Law-* West Publishing Company

Reference Book: *American Bar Association, Family Legal Guide*

Reference Book: *Historic U.S Court Cases 1690-1990*

Reference Book: *The Law Of Domestic Relations In The U.S., Second Edition, Volume I and Volume II*

Reference Book: *Family Law and Practice. Volume IV*

Index

Attorneys   48, 52, 69, 79, 81, 86

Child custody history   73, 74

Court   58, 87

Facilitator   83, 89

Family court investigator   53

Fees   69, 79

Guardian ad-litem   53

Guidelines/support   75

Judges   74

Law library   83, 89

Losing custody   66, 72

Mediation   56, 79

Non-custodial parent   75

Parenting plan   77

Paternity affidavit   78

Prosecutors office   79

Psychologist   55, 82

Visitation   77